MANY LIVES

BY

M.R. KUKRIT PRAMOJ

TRANSLATED BY

MEREDITH BORTHWICK

 Silkworm Books

ISBN: 978-974-7100-67-9

First published in 1996 by
Silkworm Books
6 Sukkasem Road, T. Suthep, Chiang Mai 50200, Thailand
www.silkwormbooks.com
info@silkwormbooks.com

Cover photograph by Pandit Watanakasiwit
Set in 11 pt. Garamond by Silk Type

Printed in Thailand by O. S. Printing House, Bangkok

10 9 8 7

ACKNOWLEDGEMENTS

This work would not have been possible without the gracious assistance of Her Royal Highness Princess Maha Chakri Sirindhorn, the advice and approval of M.R. Kukrit Pramoj and his daughter, M.L. Visumitra Pramoj; the assistance of the editors, Khun Chancham Bunnag and Achan Nitaya Masavisut; the publisher, Trasvin Jittidejarak; the Australian Embassy in Bangkok; and the unflagging support of Meredith's family, especially, her husband, John Hannoush.

The Borthwicks

CONTENTS

PREFACE

During October 17–29, 1984 I had an opportunity to visit Australia. Dr. Meredith Borthwick, whom I call by her Thai nickname, Khun Maew, was the officer from the Ministry of Foreign Affairs who accompanied me throughout the trip. Everybody was impressed with her wide range of knowledge. She spoke Thai better than many Thais. But most important of all, Khun Maew was very much her own person; she is a lovely individual.

After the visit, we often wrote to each other—in Thai, of course. Then, Khun Maew sent me a book, *The Changing Role of Women in Bengal,* (published in 1984), which was her Ph.D. thesis. Later, after my visit to India in 1987, she sent me the Thai translations of the newspaper clippings in Hindi and Bengali about my visit.

Whenever Khun Maew had a chance to come to Thailand, she always came to see me, and once even joined our New Year party. A few years ago when she and her husband, John Hannoush, were with the Australian Mission to GATT, we had tea together at the Thai Ambassador's Residence in Geneva. Their two sons were also present. Later, I gave her a call from Bern and learnt that she had cancer.

Many years ago, Khun Maew mentioned to me her translation of M.R. Kukrit Pramoj's *Lai Chiwit (Many Lives)*. She sent me the first draft, which I read and made some suggestions about.

We met for the last time on the 6th of April 1994, as Khun Maew came to Bangkok in the advance party to prepare for the visit of the then Prime Minister, Paul Keating, for the inauguration of the Thai-Lao Friendship Bridge. She told me that *Many Lives* was with the publisher in Singapore and she would send me a copy when it was published. Khun Maew also told me that she had had to resume treatment for her cancer.

Just last July, I happened to be in Paris. A friend of mine discussed her translation of the same book into French and that reminded me of the English translation. When I returned home, I immediately contacted the Borthwicks and was informed that the manuscript was then with Silkworm Books, Chiang Mai, Thailand. The family kindly let me take full responsibility for the publication of the book. I also learnt about Khun Maew's condition.

I sought the advice of Trasvin Jittidejarak, the publisher, who took over the whole publication process with her usual ability, which I much appreciated. I then asked for "official permission" for this from the author, M.R. Kukrit Pramoj, who was also gravely ill. He graciously agreed, and I thanked him for this.

Khun Maew passed away in July, as did M.R. Kukrit, in turn, three months later.

I am certain that the publication of this book will provide an opportunity for those who cannot read Thai to enjoy these stories, which present the philosophy behind much of the lifestyle of the Thai people, and it will also make M.R. Kukrit's valuable work accessible to a much larger public.

For me, this book—*Many Lives*—serves as a remembrance of

these two talented people, who had shared so many of the good things in life with me.

H.R.H. Princess Maha Chakri Sirindhorn
Chitrlada Palace, Bangkok 1 April 1996

INTRODUCTION

Many Lives, or *Lai Chiwit* in Thai, is a complex chronicle of Thai life in a bygone age, by one of Thailand's most celebrated literary figures, Kukrit Pramoj. Set in the early 1950s and first published in 1954, the work records a way of life which, for the most part, lives on only in memory. But its chief value is not as a historical record. A modern classic, it is an illuminating commentary on Thai society and its values, the pressures of change and the universality of human folly.

Kukrit's account of the genesis of the novel provides us with some insight into his purpose in writing. He recounted to this translator the incident that provided him with the inspiration for it. Some time after the second World War, during a trip to the seaside resort of Bangsaen, Kukrit and a group of journalistic friends had witnessed the aftermath of a ghastly accident. A bus had fallen over the side of a bridge. Bodies were strewn by the roadside, along with the wreckage of the bus. Official assistance was already to hand, and there was nothing Kukrit and his party could do to help. One among them was moved to reflect on what these people might have done in their lives to have brought them to this common end. The original plan was for each of the writers present to contribute one chapter, or 'life', to run as a serial in the literary monthly *Chao Krung*. Kukrit began the series with 'Loi', but when in due course the others failed to come up with their pieces, he decided to complete the story himself. It was subsequently published in book form.

Kukrit Pramoj is one of the most imposing and impressive personalities of modern Thai history. A true renaissance man, he is not only a writer of renown, as we see him here, but also politician and former prime minister, elder statesman, intellectual, journalist, classical dancer. Through these various roles, and particularly his political, journalistic, and literary careers, he has exercised considerable influence on Thai thinking. One of his major contributions is his commitment to critical thought. He has always used his lively wit and sharp intellect to question accepted norms and conventional wisdom, departing from the accepted Thai definition of a scholarly enterprise as the accumulation and reproduction of facts.

Our main concern here is with Kukrit as novelist. Even so, his personal experience is inseparable from his writings. He told this translator—and the freshness of the novel supports his assertion—that all the characters he created in *Many Lives* were drawn from experience. The gallery of personalities he had encountered on the family's feudal estates around Ayutthaya province provided his inspiration for the lives he depicted. Kukrit himself has always had sufficient financial backing not to have to depend on his literary output for his livelihood. For the most part, he would not have shared the experiences of his characters. It is a testimony to the power of his writing that he is able to depict so vividly their innermost thoughts and feelings.

I first read *Many Lives* as an impressionable teenager growing up in Thailand. Struck even then by its directness and evocative power, I have returned to it many times since, with the same appreciation. On returning to Australia in 1965, I found it difficult to share my experience of Thai literature with other Australians, as few works of Thai literature were readily available in English translation. This stimulated my interest in translation as a means of increasing understanding and bridging the cultural gap. After toying with a few other titles, I eventual-ly returned to my old favourite, and chose to translate *Many Lives*, one of the greatest of contemporary Thai classics.

While I have aimed as far as possible to render the style of the Thai original as literature, I have also tried to present the novel as a portrayal of Thai social and economic life in a particular period. I have not attempted a literal translation totally faithful to the original, but have rather tried to make the translation as readable and accessible as the original Thai. I have encountered all of the problems inherent in translating a work of this nature, including the need to explain cultural reference points, the difficulty of finding comparable terminology in many spheres, and the different cultural valuation of stylistic features. My 'solution' in most cases has been to explain where necessary and where possible without impeding the flow of the translation.

For instance, I have expanded on the chapter titles for the benefit of the English-speaking reader. In Thai, each chapter is headed by the name of the character whose life is described. Although these do not always provide a clue to the type of character portrayed, most do provide a certain amount of key information for a Thai reader. To provide similar information for readers of this translation, I have had to include in the title the profession or identity of the character portrayed, along with their name.

Meredith Borthwick

PRONUNCIATION GUIDE

The Thai words in this volume are romanized according to the Royal Institute system. A few of the Thai Buddhist terms are romanized using the generally accepted spellings, as are some names of historical people and places.

Below is an approximate pronunciation guide. In several cases, a single English spelling is used to represent more than one Thai sound.

CONSONANTS

Initial position:

K	SKIN
KH	KIN
P	SPIN
PH	PIN
T	STILL
TH	TILL
CH	JAR; or CHIN
NG	SING
R	trilled 'r' sound

All other consonants are pronounced as in English.

VOWELS

A	ACROSS, FATHER
E	HEN, DAY
I	BIT, BEE
O	HOPE, SNOW; or SAUCE, SONG
U	BOOK, SHOE; or this 'u' sound said with a wide smile

AE	HAT
OE	FUR (without 'r' sound)
IA	INDIA
UA	JOSHUA; or OE + A (as in FUR and ACROSS)
AI	ICE
AO	OUT
UI	COOING
OI	COIN
IU	FEW
EO	LAY OVER
OEI	OE + I (as in FUR and BEE)
UAI	UA + I (as in JOSHUA and BEE)
AEO	AE + O (as in HAT and HOPE)
IEO	IA + O (as in INDIA and HOPE, similar to CLEOPATRA)

PROLOGUE

THAT night, the rain poured and wind howled, raindrops crashing like solid objects onto the ground and water. A passenger boat from Ban Phaen to Bangkok, packed with people, pressed on through the current amidst the rising clamour of the rain and storm. It was late, and pitch dark. Some passengers had curled up to sleep in any space they could find; others sat hugging their knees, staring vacantly into the enveloping darkness. The sound of the rain and wind beating the canvas awning on the side of the boat almost drowned out the noise of the motor, but the boat still strained to surge ahead as if it were a living animal, goaded and beaten, dragging a load along a rough track. Voices chatting when the boat left the jetty gradually faded, overpowered by the noise of wind and rain. Only the vibrating engine showed that the boat was still moving. Occasionally someone would break the silence by yawning loudly or sighing, changing position or shifting their belongings around.

The boat passed along the river through densely-populated areas of the district town. Electric light from the sawmills on the riverbank reflected in the endless torrents of raindrops, like a curtain of water. As the boat moved past the scattered houses on the fringe of the town, towards the open fields, the wind and rain increased in intensity. Most of the passengers began to shift about uneasily, glancing at each other. At Khung Samphao junction the full force of the storm hit the boat right in the centre. People screamed and shouted; children cried in fright. Sleepers woke, startled. Everyone scrambled to grab the side that was still upright, and at that moment, the boat flung back the other way under the full weight of gravity. Then, without further warning, amidst incoherent screams and the ringing of the bell which the helmsman pulled in panic, the boat capsized. The motor puttered on for a moment then fell silent after a last violent shudder like the struggling heartbeat of a dying animal, stopped only by death itself.

The water was jet black. The storm seemed to gather strength, as if death were exalting in its victory. Voices called to each other across the darkness, but were wafted away along the swirling current. Eventually all noise ceased, leaving only the sounds of wind and rain, and the current flowing past the reeds and the roots of the sorghum grasses on the riverbank. Nature exercised its awesome powers undisturbed by humankind.

At dawn next morning the sun shone brightly down, and the raindrops lingering on the leaves and clumps of grass shimmered in the light. The glowering rainclouds of the previous night were transformed into tiny balls of fluff blown to the farthest edge of the sky. A flock of herons flew slowly over the surface of the water at Khung Samphao to gather in the field nearby. Nature had forgotten completely the rage of the night before, and was starting the new day with a bright countenance, like a child smiling through its tears.

District officials, police officers, village headmen, and many nearby residents who had come to help the victims of the previous night's disaster glanced up at the sky, then lowered their heads and went on with their bitter and tragic task.

On the bank, the bodies of the drowned were laid out in the bright sunlight. The corpses were still fresh and looked as though they were asleep. But the brisk morning air, the sound of birds chirping and settling on the bushes, and the crowing of the cock to herald the dawn would never again awaken them. Among the dead were men, women and children; young and old. There were rich men, travelling on business; some civil servants; and Buddhist monks. Their age, sex and occupation varied. Each had had a profession, life, knowledge; each had known sorrow and joy, the heat and chill of the climate, tears and laughter, love and suffering. Each had lived separately, but all died together.

Thus many lives . . . came together at one time from different places. Each life already had its own share of *karma*—whether more or less, depended on the individual. But why did all those lives have to end in the same incident, at the same time, in the same place? Many lives, yet all met the same end, death by drowning, at the same instant—a cruel blow. Could each have carried the same weight of heinous *karma*? That does not seem possible. But if we study each life separately, we might be able to discover how this course of events was ordained. We might find that the death which came to all of them was, for some, retribution for their own misdeeds; for others, a fulfilment of their wishes and a reward for determination; for some an escape, and for others merely the end to a long life. The story of these lives, now to be unfolded, forms part of the disjointed answer that ordinary mortals, lacking the wisdom of sages, can give each other.

LOI—THE BANDIT

IF anyone had asked Loi where he was born, he would have said Suphan Buri. In truth, nobody knew. The name they called him in the neighbourhood—Loi, or drifter—itself showed his origins.

One day, over thirty years ago, old Phrim who lived by the waterway rose before daybreak to put her rice pot on the fire, as was customary in that area. It was a winter morning, and she sat in front of the fire for a moment to warm her blood, which seemed to have gnarled and thickened with the cold, and to get her circulation going before she started on the daily chores. Her coarse, rough old hands, cracked at every joint from honest hard work, stretched out to the flames, and she savoured her first mouthful of betel nut for the day. At that moment she heard a child's cry in the distance. This puzzled her, as her house was in an isolated spot and was shared only by her nine-year-old nephew Thoek, still peacefully asleep under his mosquito net. She listened carefully to make sure, and heard the cries get louder. For a few moments longer she sat, indecisive. The sound was coming from the landing in front of the house. Eventually, as the noise kept getting louder and clearly was not going to stop, Phrim abandoned the fire, grabbed the flickering fish-oil lantern, and went down to the landing. By the time she got there she was convinced that it was the cry of a newborn baby, no more than ten days old. She held the lantern over the steps and saw that a clay pot had been washed up. In it was a tiny baby, screaming its lungs out as if calling for help.

Phrim felt as though her heart had stopped beating. She ran down the stairs, picked the pot up carefully, lifted the baby out, and held it close to her. Cradled in the warmth of her body, the child stopped crying and began to nuzzle around old Phrim's breast. When she put her nipple—long since dry—in his mouth, he sucked contentedly until he fell asleep. Phrim sat at the top of the stairs for a long time. She forgot the cold in the instantaneous glow of love and compassion for this unwanted babe.

At daybreak Phrim began to look around her. She stood up, and walked back to the house with the care one would devote to carrying a priceless object. Old Phrim's husband had died when she was still a girl and before she had children of her own, so she called the boy 'son'. She nurtured him, and named him Loi, meaning drift, because he had drifted right up to the steps of her landing at dawn one morning. Phrim was not to know that the creature she held to her breast was inhuman, a venomous cobra. Her warmth had revived it, but it would bite the body that had given it life and love. But Phrim would probably still have raised Loi even if she had known this. Overwhelming love can sometimes destroy the self.

Old Phrim made her living selling fruit and vegetables and other foodstuffs, such as preserved woodapple and dried goods. Every morning she set off in her boat and paddled up and down selling her produce, and returned late in the afternoon. When Loi was a toddler, her nephew Thoek looked after him at home, but by the time he was eight or nine Phrim put him to row in the prow of the boat. He was a good-looking boy, and charmed all who saw him. People who had never bought anything from Phrim's boat began to do so, attracted by the cuteness of Loi at the prow. Her business prospered. She was able to scrimp and save to buy gold to adorn her wrists, and to invest a little in fields and orchards. It was well known in the area that she was more comfortably off. Whenever anyone commented on this she would admit it and proceed to explain, "Loi brought me good fortune. My affairs have prospered ever since I took him in. He must have made a lot of merit in his past lives. I'm on my own, with no other dependents, so everything I can save will go to him. I've raised him like my own son. His own parents sent him floating off in a pot when he was just born!"

Phrim made no secret of Loi's origins, and told everyone, including Loi himself when he was old enough to understand. Maybe this was why he never felt any real ties to anyone. He was attached to Phrim, and cried when she left him, but it was cupboard love for the hand that fed him rice and gave him sweets. His feelings went no deeper than this. Thoek, whom Phrim had taught Loi to call 'elder brother', was a good-natured child, and loved Loi like his own brother. As soon as Loi was old enough, he lorded it over Thoek, who deferred to him. On the rare occasions Thoek stood in his way Loi would threaten to tell the old lady of all Thoek's misdemeanours, which forced him to back down every time.

Nine years separated Loi and Thoek: when Loi was ten, Thoek was a young man of nineteen. Yet at the age of ten Loi already seemed to have greater strength of will and intellect than Thoek at nineteen, and thus could always tell him what to do. Even so, Loi was indebted to Thoek for teaching him the skills of survival, as he was indebted to Phrim for nurturing him and giving him life. Thoek taught him how to throw bait and cast a net, where to find eels, how to use little climbing fish as bait for catching the serpent-head fish, how to trap birds and mice, and how to make wickerwork. He taught Loi to bundle the thatch for roof making, to saw and plane wood, and much else besides. Thoek was even responsible for his initiation into the differences between men and women.

One day Loi had tagged along with Thoek to help harvest the rice in the field behind the house. At midday, the rice harvesters returned for the refreshments provided for them in the shade near the threshing yard. After lunch they dispersed to the fields, sickles in hand, in the blazing sun. No-one took any notice of Loi, a mere child, so he took shelter beneath the tree with the intention of sleeping there for the rest of the afternoon. After he had been asleep a while, he heard voices chatting softly behind a nearby haystack, and with a child's curiosity, sneaked over and concealed himself behind the embankment next to it. Cautiously he stuck his head out to see who the voices belonged to. There he saw Thoek and a local girl, sitting remarkably close to each other, and they did not seem to be talking normally. Loi could not make sense of the soft sounds that were coming from their mouths, and Thoek's hands seemed to be every-where, groping and caressing beneath the navy blue farming clothes that covered the girl's body. Loi was about to yell out and tease Thoek like he always did, but his voice dried in his throat as he saw in Thoek's face and eyes an expression he had never seen before. Loi lay prone, in absolute silence. His body was as stiff as a board; his unblinking eyes stared out through the grass on top of the embankment. What Thoek and the girl did next, following the law of nature, was something Loi had never seen before but immediately recognized instinctively. His heart began to thump rhythmically. He felt a heat spreading over his face and body, hotter than sun, hotter than fire. Part of him wanted to run away, to stop watching, but his body seemed to be exerting a contrary force anchoring him to the spot. He stared fixedly at the couple, devouring the spectacle.

Just as Loi felt that his heart was going to fling itself right out of his body, everything came to an abrupt halt, like the sudden end of a storm. The girl rolled over and hid her face shyly in the haystack, while Thoek got to his knees and pulled his trousers back up around his waist. Flopping down next to the girl he nuzzled the back of her head quickly in a mechanical farewell kiss, then grabbed the sickle that lay beside him and hurriedly set off from the back of the haystack in the direction of his mates who were already reaping the rice harvest in the paddy field.

Some time later Loi slowly propped himself up to a sitting position. The girl had already followed Thoek's path back to the field, after smoothing her hair and adjusting her clothes. He felt the blood rush from his head through his body. He looked down at his clenched fists, and gradually opened the palms of his hands to reveal the clumps of grass he had uprooted without knowing it. They bore witness that what he had seen with his own eyes, and felt through the heat of his body, had actually happened. It was not an illusion or a dream.

From then on, Loi began to look at women in a broader perspective. Through the testimony of Thoek, whom he pestered constantly with questions, he learnt why men and women were born, and for what purpose. Thoek hid nothing about the condition and physical development of young men and women—he told him, and even showed him, everything. There was only one thing he did not mention, and that was love between a man and a woman. The love that binds them; that purifies lust; that calls forth sacrifice and sympathy; that makes two people into one: at nineteen, Thoek did not speak of this because he had not experienced it. At least he lacked the mental ability to explain it to Loi in words, and even if he had been able to, Loi would not have understood, because he was incapable of loving anyone in that way.

Loi's knowledge stimulated an urge to speed up his passage to manhood. He told Phrim that he wanted to grow up quickly. She shared his impatience because she wanted to live to see him ordained with the monks's yellow robe and to care for her in sickness and on death. By the time he was fifteen or sixteen, his appealing childishness began to change. He showed signs of becoming a handsome youth. The hair that Phrim used to shave for him was allowed to grow, and had a bit of a wave to it. He had sharp, flashing eyes, and the figure which had been tubby in early childhood and gangling in adolescence was now muscular, with a broad chest and shoulders, a slim waist, and a stomach as flat as a board. One day Thoek, now a fully grown man who liked his drink, said as he sat watching Loi walk back and forth, "You're so tough and strong it'd be hard to find anyone to match you. If you were a cow or a buffalo you'd fetch a good price."

On another day Uam, the village headman who often dropped in for a chat, remarked, "Watch out for yourself, Loi. You're going to be a real ladykiller when you're a bit older. If I had a daughter I wouldn't let you near the place, and if you did push your way in, I'd break your head in two!"

Whatever anyone said about him or his future, Loi continued to grow up in his own way, regardless. He claimed to be too embarassed to go selling produce in the boat with Phrim any more. She did not insist, and would have given in even if he had asked for something far greater. In fact she no longer needed to go out, as she had put aside enough in gold, money, land and orchards to give her a comfortable living in her old age, but she had done it for so long it had become a habit. She felt uneasy if she did not go, so off she went every morning, leaving Loi to stay home or roam about as he wished.

Loi spent his time observing the world, and found it endlessly fascinating. He looked on it with delight and eagerness. At times it was as if his body and mind knew, subconsciously, that he would have drifted away with the current at birth had someone not saved him. A hidden voice within him whispered constantly that his life was a gift, without initial investment, so he was at liberty to squander it. Loi did not regard this world as his, but saw it from an outsider's viewpoint, without any proprietorial interest in preserving or improving it. Seeing the world as belonging to others meant that he took no interest in whether things got better or worse. All the things in the world without exception belonged to other people; and all of them were things he desired to possess for himself. The rightful owners had better watch out, or he would take their share when they were off guard! The words good and evil had no meaning for him. The only words he believed in were to have or not to have, and everything that he did not have he would make sure that he got eventually.

When Loi was fifteen going on sixteen, his body was so well developed he looked older. He used to paddle his little boat to the market every day, moor it at the foot of the steps of the waterway in front of the market, and go up to chat and banter with friends his own age around the barber shop or the coffee house. The market near his home was a small one, selling vegetables, meat and fish, not far from the water's edge. On the waterfront there was a row of about ten wooden shophouses.

Everyone in the neighbourhood who went to buy or sell at the market soon became well acquainted with one another. Loi was a good looking boy with a cheerful disposition, who liked to clown about, so he easily became acquainted with a wide circle of people. Within that circle was one who had known Loi since childhood—the lady who owned the big grocery store in the market, *Che** Thongkham.

Che Thongkham was a Chinese woman of about thirty. She had lost her virginity to Chinaman Heng, owner of the grocery store, when she was a girl of sixteen or seventeen, and had become his wife. They had a daughter, two or three years younger than Loi, who was just blossoming into womanhood. Chinaman Heng was long since dead, and Che Thongkham had been a widow from girlhood. She had managed the store, buying and selling, in order to raise her only daughter, Suan. Che Thongkham had known Loi since he used to sit at the prow of Phrim's boat selling vegetables, so when he grew up and frequented the market she always greeted him pleasantly as he walked past her shop. He returned the greeting, as a younger person to an elder. Every time he passed he looked mean-ingfully at Suan who, being still such a girl, responded by poking her tongue out. He laughed, and did not take offence. At a later stage he put himself into Thongkham's care, and whenever he visited the market he would sit in the shop for long stretches until late afternoon or evening. During that time he waited on her readily and ran errands for her. She began to feel fond of him and allowed him to come and go as he pleased.

Friends teased him about falling for Suan, but he did not

* Literally 'elder sister' in Chinese, Chaozhou dialect. In this case it is used as a term of address referring to a woman who is Chinese.

react. Suan formed part of what he wanted, given the chance— and Loi was waiting for his chance. Yet what happened was so totally unexpected it went by undetected until nearly the end.

At midday one wet day, when the market was quiet and deserted, Loi was sitting in Che Thongkham's as usual. Suan was out, having gone off by boat that morning to visit a relative. After they had chatted a while, Che complained of aches and pains and said she was going to her room to lie down and rest her back.

"Keep an eye on the front of the shop for me," she said as she got up to go inside.

"Would you like me to massage your aches for you?" Loi asked, in the manner of a child seeking favour with an adult.

"No thanks," she said kindly, "your skill at massage might end up giving me a strained muscle."

"What do you mean? I know how to give a proper massage," Loi insisted. "Gran taught me how to when I was little, and now people are always asking me for one."

"Is that so?" Che replied hesitantly. "As you say you can, you might as well massage me for a bit then. The pain around my waist is nearly killing me."

Rain poured down. The atmosphere was dark and cloudy, as if to hide all the world's secrets. The little room became even darker, until they could only see each other in shadowy outline. Loi massaged Che, who had sunk carefully onto the mat, as if to remove all aches and tiredness from her body with the hand pressing down on her legs. Che was an elder he had to cultivate, because she owned Suan, whom he wanted. Che moaned softly in satisfaction as he pressed her legs in regular rhythm. He massaged on for a few moments before realizing that his hands had begun to squeeze her legs and flesh with unintended force. The body lying before him was no longer that of Che, but of a woman, flesh and blood and bodily heat, warm to the touch: something he had always dreamed of possessing and that he knew he would. His heart beat faster, and the blood rushed to his head as it had on the day he had helped with the rice harvest. His hands groped further, now heavily, now lightly, while Che lay with her eyes shut as if she were sleeping alone in her room, with nobody there.

A little later, in such a short time it would have escaped notice, Loi sauntered out to the front of the shop. He stood and stretched, flexing his arms and legs in a relaxed fashion. Every muscle was alive, like a hot-blooded animal. He gazed out. The rain had eased. The smell of wet earth made him take a deep breath. He knew that the rain made the soil fertile, purified the air, and filled the water jars of the villagers—filled them in the same way that his life had just been fulfilled. The level of water in the jar would fall the next day, as he knew his own sensation would, but he was untroubled. What did it matter? Rain fell, evaporated, and fell again. Thoek had often told him about these things, but his were dry tales, merely whetting his thirst. Today he learnt from Che what Thoek had tried to teach him, without the dryness, and his thirst was slaked. Loi stood and stretched again, puffing out his chest. Then he did something he had never done before. He reached out and took the lids off the glass canisters in which Che kept dry snacks like peanut brittle, preserved pomelo peel, and crisp strands of dried egg custard, and dipped his hand into this jar, then that, as if everything in the shop belonged to him. Inwardly, he was convinced that it did.

Loi dropped in at Che's store every day from then on, and stayed to eat with her. Sometimes people saw him leave late at night to go home by boat, but they thought and said nothing of it. Most of them had known him since childhood, and still thought of him as a boy. Suan seemed to have lost all attraction for him, and had there been any left, she was not what he wanted at this point. Loi's clothes, and his spending capacity, appeared to improve. His friends noticed that he had enough ready cash to treat them time after time, whereas in the past he had only managed to do so occasionally. The clothes he wore seemed newer. He graduated from cotton trousers to silk, and from old blue farmers' shirts to new ones from Bangkok. People also noticed that Che and Suan often quarrelled these days. Suan used to go off in the boat, in tears, but everyone put it down to the affectation of a girl on the threshold of adolescence.

Loi felt as though he was sitting comfortably on the pinnacle of human existence. Che looked after his every need. She provided him with as much money as he wanted. If ever she opposed him he would stay home for a couple of days, and when he returned she would give him everything he wanted, and more.

Although Loi still behaved towards others as a child, and most people regarded him as one, his consciousness was fully adult. One year passed, a second replaced it. Che was often sick. People asked her why she looked so thin and drawn, but she brushed them off. Loi alone knew that she had to take certain medicines regularly, medicines which did not prolong long-evity but destroyed a life in the process of creation, and shortened Che's life with every day that passed. Shame forced her to take it. At first Loi knew nothing of this, but in time he found out because she could not help telling him. After he learnt what was going on he used to buy the medicine for her himself, as she needed it.

In the second year, Che took the medicine for the last time. One day she lay helpless on her mat from morning, unable to stop the stream of blood. Her body was too bruised and spoiled for medicine to be effective. She lay there alone, watching her lifeblood draining away. When Suan asked what was wrong, she refused to tell her. Loi popped his head in once in the morning, but when he saw her symptoms he left the room and went fishing for the rest of the day, unmoved. Other people's lives meant nothing to him. After dark, when no-one was around, he went back to the market and crept into Che's room without being seen.

Suan sat sadly beside the lamp, which gave out a dim glow. All the doors of the store were closed except one, which was open wide enough for a person to get in and out.

"How's Che?" Loi asked, as though he were calling on a patient.

"Go see for yourself," Suan said curtly, and looked down again.

Loi entered the room where Che lay by the faint light of another lamp. He saw her lying there, her face as white as a sheet of paper, immobile, without sensation. She was breathing still, her life not yet over. The room smelt of blood.

He walked out and sat down not far from Suan. He sat for a long time without speaking, his eyes examining her from top to toe. At fifteen, she was already fully developed.

Minutes passed into hours. It was late. Loi sat motionless, never taking his eyes off Suan. The sounds of the market were silent, leaving only the croaking of frogs on the bank. Loi thought he heard the sound of movement from Che's room, and got up to take a look. She was lying stiffly, in the same position. He stretched out his hand and touched her gently on the arm. It felt cold and lifeless. He put his finger under her nose, and knew immediately that she had breathed her last. He leapt up and tiptoed lightly out of the room.

He walked past Suan without glancing at her, heading for the front door of the shop. He closed the one open door, locking it above and below, then returned to Suan. Without saying a word he took her by the shoulders and pressed her to the ground. She was shaking, her eyes wide with fright and excitement. Loi turned his head and blew out the little lamp burning beside him, and pressed his body on top of Suan's thundering heart. She lay rigid, eyes tightly shut, but she could withstand him no longer. Thus he possessed this life, to replace that which had just ended. Loi paddled his boat back home near daybreak, stretching and puffing out his chest to take in the crisp morning air from the fields with satisfaction.

The villagers in the market place were puzzled when Che's door remained closed, without a sound inside, late next morning. Friends came and called to her but there was no answer, and eventually they had to break the door down to get in. A pitiful sight greeted them. Che lay dead in her room, and Suan had hanged herself from the beam outside.

When the district official came to perform the autopsy that afternoon, Loi was among the crowd of young men who had gathered in front of the room to watch with interest.

LOI was away from home for two full years after he reached conscription age. During his time as a soldier he never ran away or broke the rules, and earned the accolade of 'model soldier' from all his superiors. In fact he thought military life, with its opportunities for travel and making friends, was fun. He regarded the daily discipline as temporary, not binding him or bending his true nature. He followed orders because he knew that if he did not, he would be jailed—he obeyed because he did not want to go to jail.

The part of soldiering that Loi really loved, like the satisfaction of an insatiable craving, was the knowledge of weaponry. He had a passionate love for all weapons destructive of human life. He loved shotguns, heavy machine guns, light machine guns, hand grenades, and grenade launchers, as a child loves its toys. He took pleasure in caressing and cleaning them. When they were taught how to take weapons apart and reassemble them, he paid close attention, missing and forgetting nothing, until he was intimate with and expert in all kinds of firearms. Loi was now an expert in firearms and shooting, just as he had once been skilled in casting the net for fish and darning it when torn. He loved weapons because they could destroy all forms of life. He had not absorbed the reasoning that weapons were for self-defence or the defence of the nation. Exhortations to be a moral person and a good citizen went in one ear and out the other, like the wind, leaving nothing behind.

After serving his term as a soldier Loi had more friends than before, all soldiers in early manhood. They came from different neighbourhoods and other villages, giving Loi the chance to travel far and wide. He was able to stay with friends in many places, because his behaviour and appearance, his consistently lighthearted manner and air of indifference to other people's business, had won him more friends than other young men of his age in the district.

One among his gang of friends was closer to him than the others. This was Thiang, a young man of the same age and village who had been friendly with Loi since their time in the army. They made a good team: Loi as master, Thiang his follower. But Thiang's people had inclinations to banditry. Bandits who robbed and plundered for a living often drank with them, so Loi had plenty of opportunity to mix with these types. Yet he kept aloof, and held back from throwing in his lot with them completely.

At that time Bandit Pruang's name was renowned throughout Loi's district. Loi knew that Bandit Pruang's camp and following were congregated at Don Mai Suk, about a day and a night's walk from his place. Bandit Pruang had extended his dominion by robbing houses within a wide radius of Don Mai Suk. No matter how the authorities tried to apprehend him, he always managed to evade their grasp. His name was known and feared by all, although most people had never clapped eyes on him and would not even have recognized him.

One day as they were drinking at Thiang's place a group of people marched into the house and called out, "Hey Thiang! Us lot have walked a long way! What are you going to give us to eat?"

Thiang looked around and raised his hands in salutation to a middle-aged man, thin and sallow, and answered, "You got this far today did you, *Phi**? Sit down, make yourselves at home— we've got loads of fish and grog, no problem."

Thiang rushed off to get supplies of drink and snacks for the visitors.

The man whom Thiang had addressed as 'phi' came over and sat beside Loi, followed by the five or six men who were with him. Loi immediately took in the fact that they were all carrying guns, but he sat impassively, not reacting in any way out of the ordinary. When Thiang returned to join the group, Phi pointed to Loi and demanded curtly,

"Who's he?"

"Oh, him! That's my old mate Loi. Don't worry, you can trust him," Thiang replied.

---

* A term used when addressing an elder brother or elder sister, and also used to address any elder person.

Phi nodded, raising his glass. The rest of the group began to talk about other things. After they had been chatting for a little while Loi began to talk about Bandit Pruang. He related the tales the villagers told about him, at great length. The men in the drinking circle glanced at each other, then at their leader. Loi was aware of their every move, but kept going as if he had not noticed. In the end the man Thiang had called Phi asked him, "Have you ever seen Bandit Pruang, Loi?"

"No, Phi," Loi replied, "I'd like to though. Given the chance I'd like to offer myself as a follower."

The drinkers laughed heartily at this, and Phi continued, "What would a good man like you want with becoming a bandit, Loi? Aren't you scared of going to jail?"

"Hell, Phi!" Loi exclaimed, "Who'd manage to catch me if I was with Bandit Pruang? But if there was a slip-up I wouldn't mind. It's in my blood—I see no point in tilling the soil and collecting fish and vegetables like I'm doing now till the day I die, without even a chance to draw breath."

"Would you like to meet Bandit Pruang, Loi?" Phi asked.

"Need you ask! I'll reward anyone who can take me to him."

Phi sat drinking silently for a time, then said, "Thiang! I'm staying overnight at your place. We'll head off before daybreak tomorrow."

Thiang turned to look at Loi and said, "Sure, Phi. Regard the place as your own—you can stay as long as you like."

"Hey Thiang!" Loi interrupted, "I'll sleep here tonight too, so I can spend a bit of time talking to Phi."

"Good idea! Don't go back. Wait here tonight and I'll introduce you to Bandit Pruang."

Loi turned to Phi, hands folded in supplication, and said, "Phi Pruang, how much longer are you going to pretend? Take me on—I'll stick it, no matter how tough. Thiang knows me well enough to back me up."

As soon as Loi let on that he knew who Bandit Pruang was, every outlaw went for his gun, but Pruang laughed and said, "You're a smart one, Loi. If you want to join me you'll have to roam around with us, you won't be able to stay home like Thiang. Do you think you can stand it?"

"I stand alone. I've got no obligations—I can go everywhere you do."

"You're on," said Bandit Pruang, "I'm going to try you out. But don't forget, when you're with me, one slip and you're dead. I don't give anyone a second chance."

Loi placed a cloth on the ground and prostrated himself before Bandit Pruang. From that day on, he was one of Pruang's men. That night there was a major robbery in the locality.

Over the next two or three years, Bandit Pruang went about looting and plundering with renewed ferocity. Before long, the villagers did not dare till their more remote fields for fear that if they had any money on them, no matter how small the sum, it would bring danger. Bandit Pruang seemed smarter since Loi joined up with him, with sharper eyes and ears. Loi quickly became Pruang's favourite. He showed himself able to plunder and rob intuitively, without guidance. And as for using weapons to kill, he did so without hesitation, as if a person were no more than a fish or a vegetable. Some of Bandit Pruang's followers behaved strangely after they had killed someone. Some would act subdued for a day, and others would get drunk. But Loi could kill anyone, child or adult, male or female. When he had finished, no matter how numerous the corpses, he was his usual cheerful self, not sad or moping. It was as if his subconscious urged him to kill, kill, and kill without exception or cessation, in revenge for the time his life was thrown adrift on the river.

Loi divided his time between following Bandit Pruang and staying at home, to avoid arousing suspicion. Phrim had aged considerably. She stayed home now, no longer able to go out by boat to sell her produce. Thoek was older too, but still un-married. Thus there were three people in Phrim's house—herself, Thoek and Loi, as there always had been. Prompted by an awareness of approaching death, one day Phrim sent for Thoek and Loi to discuss the question of inheritance. She told them to share the land, orchards, money and gold equally between them, as she had no other descendants. She made them both swear, in front of an image of the Buddha, to be loving and friendly towards each other after her death. Loi delighted Phrim by repeating the oath after her in a clear and resounding voice. Then he questioned her closely as to the various places she had hidden these valuables.

Seven days later, in the middle of the night, Phrim's house was robbed by Bandit Pruang. The robbers got hold of Phrim and Thoek, bound their hands behind them, and brutally forced them to reveal where their wealth was stored. Loi sat keeping watch at the foot of the jetty. When his mates had loaded their spoils onto the boat, he went off, armed, in the opposite direction. Phrim and Thoek were struggling, hands bound, side by side on the porch. Before they had time to work out that Loi was one of the robbers and had organized the raid on his own house, he had cocked the gun and pulled the trigger. The sound of two shots reverberated. The two bodies rolled over. Phrim was never to know that the day she divided the inheritance equally between Thoek and Loi she had, in effect, signed her own death warrant.

Late next morning, Loi came running in breathlessly as if he had just heard the news. On seeing the bodies of Phrim and Thoek lying there he burst into tears like a child, evoking the pity of the village headman and other onlookers. When he cremated the bodies of the two to whom he owed so much, some generous villagers helped meet the expenses. From then on he took possession of the house on his own.

As time passed, Loi became a respected figure in the vicinity of Bandit Pruang's Don Mai Suk. Bandit Pruang would consult him before taking any action, and all the new recruits to the band now called Loi 'brother' too. He allayed suspicion back home by saying that he was on business every time he disappeared. People believed him, and his increased wealth was proof that he was making a good profit.

One day Bandit Pruang ordered a raid on the house of the village elder at Nong Pla Khao. This time he announced that he was doing it for the sake of his reputation, because the elder not only had valuables worth tens of thousands in his house, but also had people and weapons to protect his riches. Bandit Pruang laid his plans well in advance, and when the moment came, audaciously led his band into the elder's house.

Bandit Pruang instructed Loi to take up an observation post beside a large tree away from the house, while he supervised his band to loot it. Loi waited quietly, unexcited, amidst the sound of gunfire and shouts of 'Bandit's on the prowl!' and 'Bandit Pruang is raiding!' the ritual cries his men insisted on every time they carried out a raid. Minutes later Bandit was still unable to gain entry, because of heavy fire from the occupants of the house. Two or three bullets whistled past, narrowly missing Loi. Calmly he dodged behind the big tree and stood looking out from the shadows. In the direction of the village, in the middle of the fields, he saw people milling about lighting fires and torches. He also noticed torch bearers leave the house and join forces with the others. Maybe the villagers had organized a back-up force. Shooting from the house continued uninter-rupted. Loi stood still for a second, then shouted,

"Bandit retreat!"

His cry was taken up along the line, "Bandit retreat! Bandit retreat!" In an instant, members of the robber band were running past him, cutting across the fields in a different direction from the village as had been agreed. Loi peered closely at the men running past. Even in the darkness he could distinguish the movements of each of them, yet he kept his gun cocked and remained where he was. Moments after his band had preceded him, Bandit Pruang raced past Loi, carrying his gun. Loi left a suitable interval for him to run on ahead, then put his gun to his shoulder and aimed. The sound of the shot mingled indistinguishably with the firing from the house. Bandit Pruang fell instantly, a bullet through his chest. In a flash Loi was by his side. He lifted him and whispered,

"How are you, Phi?"

Bandit Pruang, blood pouring from his mouth, rolled his eyes to look at Loi and said, "Loi! I don't think I'll be able to go on with you. Cut my head off. Don't let anyone know that they've managed to shoot Bandit Pruang."

"Don't talk like that," Loi stopped him, slinging Pruang's body over his shoulder. "Come with me, Phi, I can't leave you behind," he said, and carrying Bandit Pruang, set off in pursuit of the others.

By the time they reached Don Mai Suk next morning Bandit Pruang was too far gone to respond to treatment. He had seen the assembled faces of his band before he breathed his last, and had said for all to hear, "You didn't abandon me, Loi. Thank you."

When Bandit Pruang was beneath the ground, Loi invited the remaining bandits to have a drink with him, but they were too dispirited. Every one of them wanted to give up being an outlaw. Some wanted to till the soil, some to enter the monkhood, and, for the more infamous, to escape to somewhere they could avoid notice. But Loi tried to persuade them to stay together.

"How can we carry on, Loi?" said one. "Now Phi Pruang's dead who's going to fear us? When he was alive we only had to shout 'Bandit Pruang is raiding' for people to panic in fright. We hardly had to bother with bullets. But now he's dead, what's the use?"

"Who said he's dead?" Loi queried. "No-one knows that he's dead, apart from us here. If you'll listen to me, we can keep on making a living this way. Every time we carry out a job somewhere we'll call Brother Pruang's name, and people will be scared. That's all there is to it."

Everyone agreed, and from then on Bandit Pruang was resuscitated and launched on an even fiercer campaign of plundering and disturbing the villagers. People noticed that every time he carried out a robbery of late the owner of the property was murdered too.

LOI sat contentedly, half asleep, in the boat which left Ban Phaen headed for Bangkok. He was a fully-fledged bandit now. He could have called himself Bandit, but chose not to. He was still Loi, well known and well liked in the neighbourhood, leaving Bandit Pruang to do the robbing and be a household word. Bandit Pruang was tougher now than he used to be. He sent his men into the fray in rows, like soldiers. His weapons were better—machine guns, sten guns, hand grenades. Loi's mission to Bangkok was for the purchase of the latest in weapons, arms that could kill instantly, on target. He loved arms more than money or even women.

The sound of the storm beating down lulled Loi into a

reverie. He was unaware that the elements had already given him one chance, by ordaining that Phrim save him from drifting down the river, and that he had misused that chance and that life.

The motor boat reached Samphao junction and was about to turn. Just as Loi was thinking to himself, "My life is sheer profit," the boat turned over and sank. Loi's existence drifted away on the same current that had flown past Phrim's house thirty years ago.

When the divers found his body and laid it out on the bank next morning, Loi was smiling with broad satisfaction, as if to say, "My life is sheer profit."

SEM—THE MONK

DECADES ago, when people still travelled by paddle boat, a child was born to a wealthy family and was named Sem. Special care was lavished on him from the beginning. His parents opposed none of his childish wants, and attempted to satisfy them in so far as they could.

When Sem was still a boy running around with other children in the vicinity, adults observing the behaviour and character of the children noticed that he was not like the others. While they scampered about, laughing and shouting as children do, he stood apart, showing no sign of excitement or enjoyment. But he possessed a quality that made his friends love and follow him, even though he was no bigger than they were and never fought or bullied anyone. When smaller children who had hurt themselves or were upset came crying to him, he spoke softly to calm them and stop their crying more successfully than many adults could.

Sem differed from the others in his love and compassion for animals—all living animals, from a creature as small as an insect to one as large as a buffalo. He had never destroyed life. Whenever the other children went off to fish or catch frogs, as country children do, he played at home rather than go with them. He carefully tended any animal that had the misfortune to be hurt, for instance by a bullet, or with a wing or leg broken by a catapult, until it regained its strength, then let it go. The dogs around his place knew him well, and none had ever barked or growled or shown any signs of aggression towards him. He was able to coax even those buffaloes said to be stubborn and wayward to work as hard as their more biddable fellows.

Sem's compassion for living things increased as he grew up, along with his understanding of the sufferings of his fellow human beings. As a child, he had never understood why some of his playmates did not have all that he did. He was often puzzled when he went to play in their homes and saw that they went short of many things. Not only were clothes, bedding and utensils unevenly distributed, but in some households even food was extremely scarce. Some of his friends were thin and emaciated from hunger, their bodies covered in sores from malnutrition and lack of adequate clothing. His own family's prosperity did not make Sem rejoice at his good fortune, but instead led him to ponder on the differences in people's circumstances. At home he always found food and drink in plenty waiting for him, but there were times when the food stuck in his dry throat as he thought of his friends returning to an empty kitchen, with a lump of cold rice to assuage their hunger pangs until the next day, if they were lucky. Sometimes he brought those hungry children home with him to share his food, and watched them with interest as they ate. He could not do this very often, as the adults at home scolded him for having so many friends and being spendthrift and wasteful from such an early age. They said nothing if he brought home friends from wealthy families of similar social standing, but welcomed them liberally with sweets and cakes without a thought for the principles of thrift they had been drumming into him. Sem was astonished that those who were already of high status kept receiving more, and no-one resented it; and that people of high status were, in turn, content to accept without hesitation unlimited additions to their possessions. He was further amazed when he learned that the capacity to satisfy wants and a reluctance to impose were only to be found among the poor. He had seen children of poor parents look longingly at children of wealthy parents eating sweets, but if these were offered to them, they would squirm and refuse, or hesitatingly take only enough to be polite, without showing greed or taking liberties as children from rich families such as his would.

Sem's father, Phoem, and his mother, Klip, were looked up to by the villagers as millionaires. Having a sole heir to their name, the two of them took particular care to nurture and instruct him. Phoem drummed certain things into his son unremittingly: "Young Sem—you'll be able to get by in the future without having to work for a living because we'll leave plenty for you, but you'll have to make sure you're tough enough. I've noticed you're too kind to your friends. You'd better watch out, or when you're older, and we're dead, they'll strip you clean. Before you befriend anyone, check that they're comfortably off. You'll benefit from having well-off friends who earn a good living. At least you won't lose anything. People are poor because they're lazy, or because of their *karma*. If you start distributing things to them, there'll never be enough to go round and you'll go broke in the process. Take heed and remember this, it's my only worry as far as you're concerned."

Sem listened to his father respectfully. But he felt more uncertain each time he reflected on these precepts, because the truth that he knew, deep down, did not fit with what his father had told him. In fact it was the poor who were satisfied by a full stomach, who were grateful for even the slightest assistance and who were always ready to make sacrifices to repay their benefactors. Sem was uneasy when he thought about his father's teachings. He loved and respected his father, so on the one hand believed that he must be right. But inwardly, from his own observation of his friends' behaviour, he realized that his father had not really spoken the truth, although it would have been an unthinkable sin to have admitted to himself that his father was wrong. He was too young to know that poverty and wealth are not dependent on material conditions or amounts of wealth, but on states of mind. Poverty was like a disease buried in human nature. If it was not treated, there could be no recovery. Some rich people could be poor in spirit, and by the same token, a poor person could be endowed with wealth—not ordinary wealth, but richness of character.

Sem's confusion and bewilderment at the world increased with age. He was not so abnormal as to have been born without lust and sexual desire, or with a heart entirely free from evil. He had enough friends among young men of his own age to tempt him to seek happiness in allurements such as whiskey, women and gambling, but the enjoyment and relaxation these provided did not draw him back to them very often. At the same time, Sem noticed that as he grew into a strong young man everything he had seen as a child had begun to decline and disperse. Relatives or elders had aged and fallen ill, and some had died. The changes in everyone else's circumstances led Sem to reflect that there was little use in seeking a fleeting moment of happiness in one's youth, when that same youth was only the threshold, beyond which lay age and death. His anxiety and dissatisfaction with his present condition grew as he pondered on this. He began to seek a path to a more lasting and satisfying happiness.

The manifestation and terrifying power of death were revealed to Sem when he was about nineteen, when death came to his own household. His father fell ill with fever. His condition deteriorated, and he lapsed into unconsciousness on the fifth day. By that time, if anyone happened to speak well of any healer or doctor in any place, Sem's mother sent for them to treat the patient. However great the fee they demanded, she paid unstintingly, but money could not purchase life. His father died three or four days later. Sem nursed him up until his last breath. This was his first encounter with death. From then on, Sem believed absolutely that money and material possessions were merely embellishments to life. Money could not buy life, and had to be left behind on death.

He was alone and unsupported in this belief. After his father's death and funeral, relatives on both sides began to argue and quarrel amongst themselves over the inheritance. Sem had often seen other people's relatives quarrelling over the inheritance after someone had died, but it had never occurred to him that his own relatives would fight and compete for the spoils like everyone else. Yet after his father died his relatives contested the possession of the inheritance in exactly the same way, or possibly more fiercely, than the others. Sometimes he saw his mother crying over these matters, even more than she had over his father's death. At other times Sem worried that the villagers would hear the sharp quarrels between his relatives in which vulgar and harsh words were exchanged. Every time his mother sought his opinion, Sem gave her the only advice he could, which was to end the matter by handing the inheritance over to the others as they wished. She refused to listen, and eventually the case found its way to the courts. After a lengthy hearing in which all savings were expended in legal costs, the verdict was that the inheritance be divided amongst the relatives. The portion left to Sem's mother after the division was still enough to provide a comfortable living, but she continued to complain daily of her poverty until Sem could bear to listen no longer.

Phin was a young girl in the neighbourhood in whom Sem took a great interest. He had known her since they had played together as children. At first, he loved her as a childhood friend, but his feelings changed when they both reached adolescence. He felt an urge to care for her. When he was feeling low he only needed to hear her laugh, or to see her approaching in the distance, for his sadness to dissipate. The fires of anxiety, of fear of the uncertainties of life, smouldered constantly within him, but Phin was like the water that could extinguish those flames. When he was near her, when he could talk to her at home, meet her at the temple, or go off with her on boat trips, he was calm and happy. Sometimes he lay thinking passionately about her, and at other times he thought of her coolly, free from desire, and of the day when she would take her place beside him and he would look after her and make her happy. Phin was aware of his intentions, and at times her eyes showed that she reciprocated his feelings. She made indirect comments which led him to understand that she would one day be his. The two grew even closer, and were always together. The parents on both sides did not interfere, and the whole neighbourhood assumed that Sem and Phin had an agreement and would be partners in marriage at some time in the future.

After the death of Sem's father, Phin behaved as she always had. At first she even seemed to be trying to forge a closer relationship. But when rumours began circulating that his relatives were fighting over the inheritance, and the whole matter had to go to court, where the inheritance would be divided amongst them all rather than falling solely to Sem, she began to appear indifferent. She no longer chatted with the same familiarity, and if they met she greeted him with formal politeness rather than the spontaneous delight of a loved one. Sem did not notice this, and persisted in thinking that she had not changed, until eventually news came that Phin was engaged to the son of a millionaire from another village. Within a few days, she was married.

When he first heard the news, Sem's heart nearly stopped beating. Part of him wanted to hurt himself and put an end to his misery, but the other part was vengeful and wanted to seek out Phin and kill her, the woman he had once loved, in retribution. But these were no more than the painful thoughts of a young man, mere excrescences on the surface of a pure heart. From the deepest recesses of his being, a cool, calm voice cautioned him: "Don't do it, Sem, don't do it! Nothing in this world is permanent, not even the human heart. Have pity on living creatures! You who've never so much as landed a fish, or killed a bird—Phin is a living being. Think of it as liberating a fish or a bird!"

In the end it was the voice that won, or, to be more precise, Sem had conquered himself. Gone were his sorrow and pain, his jealousy and vengeance. Serenely, he accepted the change of heart of his loved one.

WHEN the time came for Sem's novitiate his mother took him to Wat Klang, the temple his family always went to for the ceremonial blessing of the new postulants. As people came to bless him and wish him well at the propitiation ceremony, Sem saw his mother weep with joy at seeing her son ordained. Her tears moved him more than anything. Pure tears, free from sorrow and anger and vengeance; tears full of the happiness arising from merit, not lust or the fleeting satisfaction of sexual desire, that cannot be bought by wealth and possessions. Next day, his mother bathed and anointed him with great care. After his head had been shaved, his mother's hand stroking and rubbing his body told him of her overwhelming gladness at having given birth to one about to become a receptacle for merit. Her joy, communicated through touch, pleased and gratified him. After novice Sem had been paraded back to the temple, he took the offering of robes to ask formal permission for ordination with a clear and resounding voice. At that moment, his heart was entirely free from anxiety.

During his first two months as a Buddhist monk, Sem engaged in a struggle which was the bitterest of his life, because it was a battle between an incorporeal spirit and a body of flesh and blood replete with every kind of substantial element and carnal passion. The material substance possesses heat and energy, and is likely to wield greater strength than the frail and delicate spirit, as a rule. If that spirit had no mind to engage in combat, or was a spirit easily intimidated and shamed, having but few faults, it would overlook those things which were sinful. It would see no reason for having to engage in combat with the flesh. In such a case, the owner of the body and soul might not come to experience the fatigue born of encounter. But Sem was someone whose pure heart was easily disturbed and shaken by sin, and he had therefore to fight against his body with its unbridled desires tempting him to sin so that his spirit could emerge pure and victorious.

Some nights he lay tossing with the heat of his passion. Every time he closed his eyes he saw temptations, abounding in sights, savours, smells and sounds. Sometimes he lay panting and broke out in sweat as if he had just been in a vigorous fight. On many occasions, late at night, Sem had to leave his cell and pace in meditation around the graveyard. He had to master his body, that of a young man of twenty and not to be subdued in an instant. At dawn, his body took over again, as is natural in a young man, and he had to get up quickly and hold his yellow robe close. When morning broke, he got up and hurriedly donned his robes earlier than any of the other monks. Carnal passions and desires fell away every time Sem saw or felt the robe. It was a symbol of purity, an emblem of victory respected by all, even one's parents. He knew from experience that for a person reaching manhood such as himself, the rule that the robe could only be worn between dawn and dusk not only had the effect of saving robes—scarce among monks—but also had the effect of conserving a mind and a body whose irrational demands were unbecoming to the monkhood.

Sem was a country monk, living far from civilization. Opportunities for studying Buddhist *dharma* from scholarly texts were remote. Yet Sem, his heart fearful at the prospect of evil and agonized by his own wrongdoing, became more aware of the purpose of monasticism with every passing day through careful observation of the discipline of the order. Every time he became aware that he had proved deficient with respect to particular rules, no matter how minor, he felt as if he were covered with sweat and grime and soiled with filth. He carried this sensation until such time as he could cast away his transgressions and listen to the chanting of the vows on the holy days, when he would feel as fresh and undefiled as if he had washed off all his impurities. His heart, untainted and free from sin, was the source of a happiness that Sem had never known before.

Noting that Sem had been a monk for less than one wet season, some lay people would tease him and ask, "What do you think of being a monk? Is it better than a householder?"

He would answer, "I feel much better. I've only ever taken a bath since I've been a monk."

The lay person would look at him in astonishment and ask, "Hey! Why is that? Didn't you ever bathe before?"

"Yes, I did, every day, many times a day. But bathing as a layman was just bathing the outward parts, getting rid of a few spots of dirt. It is only since my ordination that I've found a way of bathing that is totally cleansing."

The lay person would then look at Sem apprehensively and change the subject.

When Sem had been a monk for one wet season, his mother came and asked him to return to the laity on the auspicious day and time she had arranged for him. He agreed passively. Until then he had not thought beyond his intention to be a monk for one season. As the day for leaving the monkhood approached, however, he began to feel a yearning for the monastic life such as he had never felt for anything else before. When the time came to rejoin the laity, Sem felt scared and repelled by the prospect of life without precepts or peace. He felt as though he was about to step from a cool place into the flames of a bonfire. He was often preoccupied and uneasy in the days leading up to his departure from monkhood.

His mother arrived at the temple early, with her offerings for the monk. There were white robes for him to change into for the leave-taking, and another set of clothes for him to wear home. A number of monks who had been ordained with him were due to leave the same day. While they were laughing and teasing relatives, as young men do, Sem sat quietly, his head bowed. His mother looked across at him in puzzlement many times.

When Sem's turn came to kneel and take his leave before the assembly of monks, he moved forward and knelt motionless with his hands joined in prayer. He tried to force himself to say the words "I leave the monkhood". Only four words, but they would not come. The assembled monks sat before him in complete stillness, eyes lowered, waiting in passivity and detachment for him to announce his leave-taking. Their yellow robes bathed their skins in a golden radiance. Their faces and eyes reflected abiding, motionless peace, suspended in a place where Sem wanted to be, clad in the yellow robe he wanted to be wrapped in when he died. He cast his gaze over the assembled monks as if to ask for their help, to cling on to him and not to let him drift back to the desires and passions of the world. But not one of them caught his eye or showed any other lapse of discipline. His lay relatives, waiting for him, fell silent. They stared in suspense as they waited for the words announcing his departure from the monkhood to pass his lips. He made another effort to get the words out, but failed. It was as if he were floating, with blocked ears and blurred vision.

Sem bent his knee, hands folded and eyes shut in stillness, for another moment amidst complete silence, then made a move. He reached out and pulled the robe and wrapper tightly around him, as if scared that they would blow away. Turning towards the image of the Buddha, he prostrated himself three times. Then he crawled backwards, away from the assembly of monks, to remain in the monkhood. When he was sufficiently far away, he stood up, and walked through the group of lay people who sat immobile, staring at each other in astonishment. He walked back to his cell, closed the door, and bolted himself in alone.

Sem remained in solitude in his cell until evening. During his time alone he dedicated himself to the Buddha and vowed silently that he would stay in the monkhood until death. He would try to find a way of lessening all suffering and sorrow, for as long as he lived. He knew that the world was full of suffering, but he also knew that opportunity to lessen it would be rare and his capacity to do so limited. Sem felt the relief of one lost in the dark, for whom someone had lit a flame to light the way. Doubts, anxieties and worries that had assailed him in the past left him. His path was clear, and he would tread it with confidence and without fear.

Late in the afternoon Sem opened the door of his cell and came out. His mother was waiting at the foot of the stairs. Her sorrow showed on her face. Seeing him, she greeted him with hands folded in salutation, tears pouring down her cheeks. She beseeched him to leave the order and return to set up house, to be her succour in her old age. Sem sat and listened quietly to her in a spirit of detachment.

"Mother, I have made up my mind," he said at last, "that I will don the yellow robe until death. Although you are getting old, I can still look after you as a monk, and repay the care you have taken over me. Don't worry on that score."

She began to weep loudly, saying, "Now don't think I'm just a miserable sinner—but if you don't come out, then who's going to look after the house, and the orchards and the land? Won't they all fall out of our hands? I'm old, how much longer will I be around? Please, leave the monkhood. This much study will have earned you as much merit as you'll ever need. How much more do you want? Do leave. We've got enough to live on for the rest of your life, you won't have to work hard for a living. I'll find you a bride—a good, pretty, girl—whoever you like. Never mind how much they ask—I'll gladly hand it to them on a silver platter, as long as you're happy."

Sem sat and thought about all the things his mother was describing. The world considered these desirable: money, property, wife, children, orchards, fields. They were sought after by everyone. Some earned them by dint of hardship and sacrifice; some came by them through trickery and deception, or even plain robbery and plunder. His mother could not know how much he had changed. One season in the monastery had made Sem's heart grow in purity like a seed sown on rich soil. Her descriptions might have persuaded others to leave the order of their own accord, but those same things made Sem reluctant to leave. If being a layman meant setting up house and jealously guarding wealth; if being a husband and father meant having loved ones who would eventually be taken away; then he had no desire to be a householder, a husband or a father. In the short time he'd been within the orbit of the yellow robe, he had glimpsed true peace and happiness many times. He knew, too, that there were mysteries and light in the *dharma* that had not yet been revealed to him. He wanted more of these—they led him to seek further for the truth. Sem sat and pondered these matters thoroughly and then said,

"I've made up my mind, Mother. You go on home. I'm not leaving."

His mother wept out loud, like a child, and sat sobbing for a long time. Finally she realized that nothing she could say would shake his determination, and taking her leave, she departed for home in despair, utterly dispirited.

OVER the next three years, Sem threw himself into religious activities as young men of those times were trained to. He was eager for supernatural powers, and believed that he might acquire these through strict self-discipline. He began to memorize various magic spells and to collect magical objects. Whenever he heard of a monk possessing spells for immortality or for compassionateness, he pledged himself to their service to learn their techniques and spells until he had committed them to memory. If he heard of a temple which had amulets or talismans, he tried to get to know people there to get hold of these. From day to day, Sem spent his spare time in his cell sanctifying these objects, and himself, with magical powers. He sincerely believed that these methods would eventually lead him to the final goal. Sometimes he became so engrossed he sat reciting spells until late at night, and after a while became emaciated from lack of food and sleep, and from anxiety over his spells. He began to look like someone with chronic fever, with wandering eyes which avoided one's gaze, like a madman. At times he stuttered and stumbled in his speech. It reached a point where the rest of the monks in the temple became concerned about him. But no-one dared give him advice because they were reluctant to discourage what they believed to be meritorious practices.

Sem was brought to his senses by something from an unexpected quarter. An old man used to bed down each night in the riverside shelter of the temple pavilion. The monks and local people called him 'mad old Chom', because he used to laugh at things other people did not consider funny and sometimes talked in a way that no-one could understand. He had few possessions other than a broken-down boat in which he did the rounds begging from house to house, a cracked cooking pot, a stove and a few chipped cups and plates which were his culinary equipment, and a marijuana pipe, his favourite object. Old Chom stayed at the pavilion and, like a bird, came out every morning to look for food. He headed off in his tacky boat and returned in the evening. At night, when he was pleasantly high, he visited the monks' cells and took the liberty of drinking hot water and tea with them and chatting to any of the monks or novices who cared to speak to him.

One night mad old Chom poked his head into Sem's cell and asked, "What's the matter with you?"

"Nothing," Sem replied, "I haven't been sick, just a bit worn out, that's all."

"If you're tired and ill, why not try sleeping in the temple for a bit?"

Sem said, "It's peaceful at night, so I sit and recite incantations."

Old Chom persisted, "What do you want with recitation?"

"Well, I recite the spells I've learnt, partly for my own satisfaction, partly to consecrate amulets. I like experimenting with that kind of thing. They say if you do it properly you'll become invulnerable, and invisible, and be able to walk on air, but I don't know yet because I've just started—I might not be doing it right."

Old Chom cackled gleefully and remarked, "Become invulnerable! Make yourself invisible! My, you're really going in for learning! And who do you need to be invisible from? Are you so afraid of someone that you have to become invisible to escape? And if you could walk on air, where would you go? There are barges around, why not go in comfort?" And with that, Old Chom wandered away laughing, leaving Sem to sit alone and ponder the wisdom of his remarks.

From then on, the spells lost their meaning. Sem had learnt from Old Chom that even if they worked, they were useless. A monk like himself had no need to take up the cudgels with anyone. His yellow robe was adequate protection. Everyone who saw it paid obeisance to it, and entertained no thought of harming him. He had no reason to fear anyone enough to need invisibility, because everyone welcomed him gladly—a disciple of the Buddha. As for walking on air, that was hardly necessary for one who lived simply in any surroundings, and had surrendered all need to rush and hurry. He began to eat and sleep at the usual times again, like the other monks. His skin shone with an extra radiance through the denial of yet another temptation.

Even though he now lived as an ordinary monk, no longer interested in spells and such things, Sem soon became aware of certain compulsions. Merely living from day to day, even observing the precepts, did not satisfy him. He wanted to reach a goal, a goal he had not formulated clearly yet. He was certain only that he would know when he had attained it.

He had heard of some ascetic monks, who studied human corpses and skeletons and only ate one meal a day. Even this was all mixed up without regard for sweet and savoury, to overcome the sensation of taste. Sem had not tried this path, and began to follow it. He subjected his body to extremes. He gave up his daily begging round and began to eat rice with banana, salt, and tamarind juice, mixed with bitter leaves. He ate this out of half a coconut shell. Worse, he searched the burial ground and found a skull from a pauper's corpse to put beside his bed and contemplate at every opportunity. He did all this for many months, but the desired result was not forthcoming. On the contrary, he wasted away and became vague, unable to look people in the eye, as had happened once before. Eventually mad old Chom saw that Sem looked as though he was heading for trouble. Chom wandered up to Sem's cell one day at noon as he was eating his rice mixture from the coconut shell.

He sat and watched for a moment, then asked, "What are you eating?"

"Rice."

"Why do you have to eat it like that?"

"So that I take no pleasure in the taste of the food," Sem explained.

Old Chom laughed loudly and said, "You are strange! When

you think about it, you have to beg for food just like me, but you're luckier, because you have a choice. If I were to choose to live on rice and bananas and tamarind water I'd be in trouble, because if no-one gave it to me I'd end up starving to death. I have to take what I get, I can't be as fussy as you. I have to eat just what I'm given. Oh well."

Old Chom sighed deeply, and peered into the cell. Seeing the skull, he said, "What've you got that skull there for?"

"It's to help me to a realisation."

"What realisation?"

"The realisation that we are all born to die, decompose and decay, as a matter of course."

Old Chom turned and looked at Sem, and questioned him further. "Does it take this skull to make you realize that once born we have to die? You shouldn't forget so easily! Everybody has to die. Skulls and ghosts are best left in the graveyard, not brought to your bedside to clutter up the cell!" Having said that, Old Chom left, muttering to himself.

Once again, Old Chom's conversation left Sem feeling ashamed of himself. It was true, the word *bhikkhu* meant 'one who begs', and in his position he should not be choosy. The decision to eat only a particular kind of food was in itself a fault, creating wants and needs where they had not previously existed. The skull he kept by the bed as a perpetual reminder of death was the same. This was basic knowledge, and not to know it could only be wilful ignorance. Sem knew that as a monk he had less excuse for such negligence than other people, so these petty reminders were in fact an unnecessary luxury.

From then, Sem gave up the practice of extreme asceticism and turned seriously to meditation. He tried concentrating on entering into a trance, but failed. He experimented with sitting in deep meditation, with putting green objects in a circle, and with concentrating on a round hole pierced in paper to radiate light. Sometimes he sat in front of a candle and directed his thoughts and emotions onto the flame. He experienced strange sensations and saw weird apparitions. He felt lightheaded. His ears blocked and produced a floating sensation. He saw bizarre configurations—a hell full of ghosts and demons, or heaven with its deities. At first he was pleased to see such things, but he was old enough and sensible enough not to be seduced. He knew that these were the images of temple murals, the only difference being that his gods and goddesses could move. Otherwise the details were identical: the gods dressed the same way, and the place was that depicted on temple walls; the demons were similar, with nothing beyond what could be seen in the murals. Sem examined the murals thoroughly and compared them with the apparitions he saw in meditation. He was convinced that his visions were not really of heaven and hell, but an illusion, springing from the recesses of his own subconscious memory.

He persisted, despite this knowledge. But the marvel of peace is that it can only be attained on the cessation of seeking. The more one wants to attain it, the further one is from the goal. As everything Sem did was governed by a desire for attainment, his goal eluded him. Yet his determination was not a hindrance, but a preparation for entering into states which few people ever approached.

One night after bathing Sem was preparing for bed. He lit candles and incense to make obeisance to the Buddha and recite his daily prayers. The candlelight fell on the face of the little Buddha image, illuminating it. Sem glanced at it, and, struck by the beauty of the radiant image, meditated on the characteristics of the Buddha. His satisfaction deepened as he reflected. He recited the common prayer 'I take refuge in the

Buddha' over and over again, with no particular objective. Through his concentration on the Buddha's qualities, all desires and temptations fell away. Sem was fully aware that he had not soared into another realm but was sitting in front of an image in his cell. But he was in a state of perfect concentration. A radiance illuminated his cell, a cool quiet light that came not from sun or fire, a self-luminous light unlike the reflected light of the moon. He felt overwhelmingly happy, with an enlight-ened happiness resulting from surrender. It was not the surrender of the senses, though, but the bliss of the complete extinction of desire.

Sem could not recall how long he sat there. Eventually he came to his senses, and the light disappeared. The candles and incense had long since gone out. That night Sem went to bed with a sense of fulfilment he had never before experienced.

SEM proceeded to practise his religion with an inner confidence, untroubled and free from striving. He looked on the world with kindliness and without curiosity. All life was worthy of compassion, because all life was suffering. All living creatures shared his suffering, and were thus objects of his compassion, and the power of his compassion made others reciprocate. Animals loved Sem more than anyone. Even the wild birds that took refuge were not afraid of him. Instinctively, they felt he would do them no harm. His reputation for compassion toward humanity and animals spread.

He acquired a name for holiness, and after twenty years in the monkhood, attracted a large following. By the age of forty, people called him *Luang Phi* (reverend brother) or *Luang Lung* (reverend uncle), as was customary among village folk. An incident that took place around that time gave him a reputation for exorcising ghosts and demons, and for curing ailments created by their evil spells.

A new family had set up house by the bank of a waterway not far from the temple. Sem had childhood memories of the ruined house that had previously occupied the site. When the new house was built all traces of the ruin were razed, except for a few stumps which had been the foundation posts. The new family built their house away from the old stumps, but put up a buffalo pen near the ruins. Their twelve-year-old son, Dan, was a nice, well-mannered boy. Sem knew him well, as Dan was often sent over to the temple with things for him. One holy day at the full moon Sem had seen him playing round the temple when his parents came to make merit, but a few days later he had word that Dan had come down with a strange illness.

Dan had been to fuel the fire for the buffaloes in the pen on the night of the full moon. He returned crying, and complained of pains. He barely ate or drank, but sat staring at the buffalo pen, and frequently burst into tears. His parents had to calm him to get him to eat, but he ate so little he became dangerously emaciated. When his parents asked him why he was crying he refused to answer, because at first they had not believed what he told them and had accused him of being delirious with fever.

At first Sem took no particular interest in Dan's illness. He thought it was just an ordinary fever. But after Dan had been missing from the temple for nearly a month Sem asked the villagers what had happened. They told him that Dan was possessed, and would probably die soon. His father had had a number of folk healers and physicians to treat him, but he was getting worse. Sem was sorry to hear this, because Dan was still young. One day, after lunch, he took a boat and called on him at home.

Dan's parents were pleased to have a monk visit him, and took Sem into Dan's bedroom. Sem was moved by pity when he saw Dan's emaciated state. He sat beside Dan and gently stroked his forehead, with compassion. Dan opened his hollowed eyes. When he saw Sem he called softly to him, "*Luang Pho* (reverend father)."

"What's wrong with you, Dan?" Sem asked.

Dan looked at his parents and burst into tears, saying,

"Luang Pho, I feel sorry for him."

"He's raving," his father said anxiously.

"Leave him to it," Sem said, and asked Dan, "Who do you feel sorry for?"

"I don't know, Father, but he came crying, pleading for his life, that night at the edge of the buffalo pen. I heard him with my own ears. It was pitiful, a cry for life—it's still ringing in my ears. I feel so sorry for him."

Sem looked to Dan's father, who responded, "It's the spirit's doing, Luang Phi. When Dan first told me, I went out and sat there myself for a few nights, but nothing happened. I told him, but he won't believe it."

"I really did hear him, Reverend Father," Dan said softly, his eyes fixed on Sem. "Help him, Luang Pho, I feel sorry for him."

"When did you hear this voice?" Sem asked.

"On that holy night of the full moon, Luang Pho," Dan replied. "I can remember, because it was a clear full moon night. Help him, Luang Pho. He was begging for life."

Sem sat thinking. It was the thirteenth day of the waxing moon, and in two days it would be the holy day of the full moon. After a moment's consideration he said, "Don't worry Dan. Have something to eat and drink or you'll feel worse. I'll come back on the night of the full moon and do what I can." A few minutes later he returned to the temple by boat.

Sem returned to Dan's on the holy fifteenth day of the waxing moon, by the light of the now full moon, as he had promised. Dan was awake, and his parents explained that he had been waiting. He looked hopefully at Sem, who told Dan's father to carry his son from his bed down to the buffalo pen where he had heard the strange voice.

That night everything was clearly visible. The full moon floated above the horizon. The few buffaloes in the pen lay peacefully chewing their cud. All was still, apart from the insects and the monotonous croaking of the frogs in the waterway. Sem asked Dan's father to sit Dan on his lap by the pen. He himself stood close by, waiting to hear the voices Dan had described. The stumps of the old foundation posts, the ruins of the old house Sem had known as a child, stood before them. Moonlight touched the posts and cast a shadow along the ground.

Sem stood quietly for a while. As the moon rose, the shadow from the posts retreated, and a voice piped up from around the old ruins. It was the sound of a young boy crying, a chilling, haunting wail of fear or terrible grief. Dan began to sob as soon as he heard it. His father started in fright, and made as if to run away.

"Don't worry, I'm still here," Sem reassured him, and stepped from the edge of the pen into the full glare of moonlight, towards the sound. The voice cried even more, and said in a frightened tone, "Mother, open the door . . . Uncle is going to kill me. Uncle, spare me, spare my life. I'll give you anything . . . just spare my life. Mother, open the door!" This was followed by wailing, interspersed with repeated cries for his mother to open the door.

The area was completely open, with no bushes or trees where

anyone could hide. Sem looked around carefully. The voice was unmistakably human. Fear, or attachment to life, had bidden it to sound long after the corporeal remains of its owner had gone. Sem's heart overflowed with compassion, and he called, "Why are you crying? The cause of your unhappiness has been gone for a long time. Be still!"

The voice became softer, the sobbing less violent.

"Everybody else has gone to their chosen place. Stop your crying and pleading for life—no-one around here would dream of harming you."

The voice vanished, along with the sounds of the crickets and frogs.

"You've paid for all your previous sins and *karma*. Go, and be born again in your chosen place. Now, repeat what I say," Sem declared into the void. Clouds had drifted over to hide the moon, plunging the area into darkness.

"I take refuge in the Buddha."

Sem had begun the Pali chant of the triple gems. A few seconds later the voice repeated, "I take refuge in the Buddha."

"I take refuge in the *dharma,*" Sem continued, followed by the voice.

Sem recited the triple gems three times, and each time the voice echoed him. A cool breeze wafted by, carrying the sound of gentle laughter mingled with relief. A cloud formation had passed over the moon. Brightness reigned once again. Sem nodded to Dan's father to carry the boy home, and then took a boat back to the temple.

Dan recovered rapidly, and Sem's reputation for healing and exorcising spirits spread far and wide.

FAITH is like a virulent strain of infection. The germs exist in abundance in every heart, and are like bonfires which burst into flame as soon as someone applies a match. Sem's fame spread like wildfire. Instead of calling him 'Luang Phi' or 'Luang Lung', they called him 'Luang Pho'. Everyone had heard of him, from the district of Chao Chet, Suphan Buri, all the way to Ayuthaya. People flocked to his cell, asking for consecrated objects. At first he had nothing to give them, and told the lay people who came to him, "Despite what everyone says, I don't have any consecrated objects to give you."

But the faithful refused to believe him, and stood firm in their demand. Sem accidentally let slip, "If you don't believe me, see for yourself. There's nothing in this cell apart from an old under-robe and a tray full of tea leaves that the novice put out to dry."

With that, they instantly ripped the robe apart and divided it. The tea leaves vanished in a second, shared out by the handful. They brought the bits of cloth and tea leaves to Sem for blessing. To avoid an uproar, he fixed his mind in a state of compassion and took the objects in his hand while concentrating on the Buddha. Then he returned them to the claimants, with the precept, "Show compassion for all living beings, oppress no-one, and live in harmony with others."

The shreds of robe and tea leaves became sacred objects. Every day more people offered to be his disciples. Each asked for a piece of cloth or a handful of tea leaves as a talisman, renowned for effectiveness in compassion. Those who had got hold of them were reputed to have fulfilled their wishes and dissipated all enemies and ill feeling towards them.

One day the leader of the monastic council for the region, having heard of Sem's reputation, came by boat from the temple in the district town. Even though he was many years younger than Sem and his junior in monastic life as well, he had attained the title *Phra Khru* (venerable teacher) through his studies in Buddhism. Sem received him and ungrudgingly accorded him due respect. After exchanging politenesses, the Phra Khru asked, tongue in cheek, "They say you have sacred objects."

Sem laughed and said, "It's nothing really, just a few bits of old robe and tea leaves. Everyone took them and brought them to me to consecrate, so I obliged."

"And what did you say?"

"I offered compassion, recited the triple gems, and meditated on the Buddha, that's all. And when I gave it to them I told them to have compassion for all living creatures and not to oppress each other."

The Phra Khru stayed a few minutes to ask after his health and well-being, then took his leave. Before doing so he fell to his knees and prostrated himself three times, saying, "Luang Pho, I too beg for a piece of your robe as a momento. Anyone who can follow your teaching—showing compassion to all creatures without oppressing others—will prosper and live in happiness."

And that was so. Those who presented themselves as followers and took consecrated objects away with them observed Sem's teachings. They showed compassion to all, did not oppress others, attained happiness and prospered. Their enemies really did disappear. Many of his followers thus became quite affluent. Sem's fame brought him material wealth. Some gave him costly gifts or tasty foods. He took no notice, and passed what was given on to more needy monks or gave it as alms to the poor. He never deviated from this practice.

TWENTY years later, Sem's seniority made him abbot of Wat Klang. He had countless followers, who were at one in their puzzlement over the unimproved state of the temple.

Everything in it was in good repair, but the chapel was made of old bricks, the teaching pavilion was of wood, and the cells were still the kind with thatched roofs that everyone remembered from their childhood. The surrounding temples had changed beyond recognition, with concrete halls, chapels, and jetties of various sizes. The cells now were made of brick, interspersed with schools for preachers, large rainwater tanks, bell towers and so on. Brightly coloured glass adorned everything, inspiring aesthetic pleasure in the beholder. Someone had once asked Sem why his temple, with its steady stream of devotees, did not share the brilliant condition of others. He answered, "It seems to me that monks can only survive as servants of lay people, or to put it simply, by depending on them for our daily bread. I don't want to destroy anybody's faith, but as long as the people live in houses with thatched walls and roofs, without protection from wind or rain, I don't want to be in a brick house. When anyone wants to donate money for the temple, I tell them to take it back to build a house with timber walls. I'll only think about having brick walls when every villager has them."

ONE day, when Sem was about sixty, he felt a painful itching sensation on his right cheek, at the jaw. Feeling it, he came across a lump the size of a match head. He covered it with a wax ointment, but it swelled and began to ache. Some nights it ached so much he could not sleep, and he would have to get up and meditate until the pain disappeared. But as soon as he came out of his trance-like state it returned. As time went on it began to ache at regular intervals, day and night. Sem's old body became uncharacteristically gaunt, while the lump on his jaw broke into a sore, like a gash from an elephant's tusk. He had difficulty eating, and when he drank the water seeped out through the gash, a piteous sight. Sem took stock of himself and realized that his time had come, but he remained calm and behaved as he always had. His less enlightened followers became uneasy and worried, and called in numerous doctors to treat him, but the symptoms would not go away. The doctor at the municipal clinic delivered the final verdict. Sem had cancer, and would have to go to Bangkok for examination and treatment.

His followers came in a body to plead with him to go to Bangkok. He resisted initially, but when he saw their anxiety he agreed to go to allay their worries.

SEM travelled by small boat with a number of acolytes, and changed to a larger one at Ban Phaen for the journey to Bangkok. As the boat left the pier the pain started up again, more acutely. It hurt so much, it was as if there was a live animal in his jaw, eating away at the flesh. While the boat sailed through the wind and rain, Sem began to go into a trance to raise his mind above his tortured body to a more peaceable realm, free from the desire that was an even greater agony than the cancer.

Had Sem struggled like the others when the boat went down he would still have perished, as he was sitting in the special elevated section reserved for monks at the back of the boat, away from everyone else. Nevertheless, at the moment it sank, his mind was released from the body and all corporeal sources of sorrow, and he had no inclination to struggle to retain his grip on the roots of suffering.

When his body was retrieved the next morning, everyone marvelled to see that he was still in the posture of Indra's thunderbolt, or the diamond position. The purity and fullness of his existence had led the god of death to spare him the agony of a protracted illness. The peaceful life paused, then halted, in the water with a coolness which was like water itself. Sem had been swept out on the current to the sea, never to return to the cycle of birth and death.

PHANNI—THE PROSTITUTE

IN fact, her name was not really Phanni at all. That was just the alias or trade name that she used professionally. She remembered that from her earliest days, her mother and others who knew her called her Roen. She started using the name Phanni later, after she had come a long way from home.

Phanni remembered that when she was little she had lived at Ban Phaen, at the edge of a field, quite a long boat trip away from the Sena district. Her mother was called Riu, and had named her only daughter Roen. Phanni did not know who her father was. Every time she had asked, Riu would shout and abuse her, as if the word 'father' was a fuse which triggered off a massive explosion of suppressed resentment.

When Phanni reflected on her childhood she found that she only had a hazy recollection of anything other than poverty. Poverty was the only detail of life that mattered, and was imprinted so deeply on her consciousness that it eclipsed traces of more superficial details. She knew that she had lived in an old shack with her mother, Riu, and that the two of them had lived alone, without any other family and without any possessions other than their own poverty-stricken lives. Riu never explained why they were so poor, but she intended to hang onto the two items left to her—her life and that of her daughter Roen—as best she could. As her own labour was her only resource, Riu took on any work, light or heavy, as long as it paid her a living wage from day to day. Poverty was a bridge to death, because starvation was always waiting at the gate. Riu seemed to expend all her energy working to stave off that kind of death.

Phanni remembered that she had tagged along with her mother, wherever she found work. Sometimes, catching sight of her daughter's face when she had been working at some particularly backbreaking job, instead of feeling heartened and rejuvenated Riu would say resentfully, "Child of fate! Why were you ever born! You're just an extra mouth to feed." If Phanni cried, or showed that her mother's curses frightened her, Riu would scold even harder, beat her, and push her around. Abuse and bashings were a fact of life. They no longer affected her, mentally or physically. Yet even though Riu showed her no affection, Phanni always remembered that she had once loved her mother with unparalleled devotion, and when she grew up she could not recall ever having loved anybody or anything more than that. The force of love is in everyone, and individual love seeks out the most promising object in any given environment. While Phanni was still a child, Riu was the best and closest object.

Like mud collecting on the wheel of a bullock cart, poverty took greater hold of her life as she grew older. No matter what she asked for, her mother would answer immediately, "No! We're too poor! We've barely got enough to eat!" She became accustomed to this response and eventually provided it herself, unprompted. Everything was prohibited. "No! We're too poor," was the phrase she heard and pondered over with greatest frequency.

When Phanni was little her mother took her along to work with her. She did not know who she could leave the innocent child with, as she was totally alone and had no relatives to fall back on. By the age of five or six, however, Phanni stayed back at the old shack, because Riu believed that she could look after herself. Phanni also had to do the housework, and if she went off and played instead, as children do, Riu thrashed and abused her, invoking poverty to justify her actions.

Phanni lived with poverty—past, present and future—until one day, when she was nine years old, Riu took her to a big house, between the market and the district office. Phanni had no way of knowing whose house it was, but she saw that it was large and prosperous and occupied by a great number of people. Riu made her sit on one side of the verandah while she went in to speak to a middle-aged woman whom Phanni had heard people calling *Khun Nai.** After speaking to Khun Nai for a moment Riw beckoned to Phanni to come and sit next to her. She heard Khun Nai's voice saying, "She's cute looking! I'll bring her up as my own child. I haven't got any daughters. If I get her I'll take very good care of her."

"Yes ma'am," Riu replied, "I'm very poor. See it as an act of kindness to a baby crow or bird, I beg you."

"How much?" Khun Nai asked.

"Only eighty ma'am."

"What do you mean, eighty!" Khun Nai exclaimed. "I offer to take your child and raise her well and you've got the nerve to ask for eighty? Let's not have any of that!"

"It's up to you then, ma'am," Riu said weakly. "I'll take whatever you offer, I won't argue about it."

"Fifty," said Khun Nai, "That's my only offer. Take it or leave it."

* A form of address meaning 'mistress of the house'.

Riu turned and looked at her daughter, with trembling lips. For the first time, her expression showed a trace of love and regret. But ultimately, she decided to turn back and close the sale of her daughter to Khun Nai for fifty baht. Khun Nai counted out the money, and Riu took it, her hands shaking. She had not received this much money for a long, long time. Then she left, but not before one last instruction to her daughter: "You stay here with Khun Nai, Roen, and when she goes to Bangkok you go too."

After Riu had left the house and gone, Phanni sat crying on the edge of the verandah. She dared not run after her because she knew that she would be beaten. She looked around at the other people in the house, but they were all strangers. Feeling scared and awkward and not knowing what to do, she just sat there crying.

"Come here!" Khun Nai called out to her in a frighteningly decisive tone. Phanni stood up and walked towards her.

"Look at you! No manners at all!" Khun Nai cried. "In future when I call, don't walk—crawl, and don't forget."

Phanni sank to her knees. When she got close to Khun Nai all she could do was sit with her head down, not daring to look up. Khun Nai reached over, with icy fingertips that startled her, and took her by the chin to lift her face up.

"You're not bad looking, but so dirty," Khun Nai said, and went on to ask, "What's your name?"

"Roen," she said.

"Roen, Khun Nai," Khun Nai corrected her in a commanding voice.

"Roen, Khun Nai," Phanni echoed.

"Lamai, Lamai," Khun Nai called to someone inside. A woman replied "Yes, Khun Nai," and came out, on her knees.

"Give this girl a bath, and find some old clothes for her to change into. She stinks!" Khun Naiordered, and went into the house.

The woman called Lamai took Phanni to bathe at the foot of the jetty. While she was bathing, the woman grumbled softly, as if to herself, "She must be ill-fated, poor thing. What kind of person would sell their own dark-eyed daughter—and not just to anybody, but to that hard-hearted ogre."

Phanni started her new life with Khun Nai with mixed feelings. On the one hand, she missed her mother, and her old surroundings, which she knew meant poverty. On the other hand, she was excited at the prospect of a new life, happier and more comfortable than the old. She had not forgotten that Khun Nai had purchased her as a daughter, and that her mother had said that when Khun Nai returned to Bangkok, she was to go too. Phanni noticed the change in her circumstances the very first night she came to live with Khun Nai. Even though the side dishes at the evening meal that Lamai prepared for her were drier and fewer than she ate at home, the amount of rice was limitless. She could eat as much rice as she liked, and for the first time, she felt that she had eaten her fill.

Two or three days later Phanni went to Bangkok with her owner Khun Nai, who now exerted the rights of possession over her life. Her first glimpses of Bangkok excited her: the tall buildings and big houses, the wide streets, heavy traffic and masses of people made her agog with wonder. She forgot all about her early surroundings. She looked at Bangkok with craving, because it seemed replete with everything worth seeing and having. Childlike, she thought to herself that even if you roamed it from youth to old age you would never see all of a place like Bangkok. Back home, she had always been pleased when her mother took her to the market, even though there it was only a single row of shophouses and not as good as the district market. But after she had seen Bangkok, the district market was nothing. The only thing wrong with living in Bangkok was that Khun Nai would not let her leave the house. Even though such a wealth of entertainment awaited her outside, Phanni could only stand and watch from inside Khun Nai's gate.

If the truth be known, there was enough going on inside Khun Nai's house to fill Phanni with wonderment. She had never, in all her born days, dreamt or imagined that ordinary people could possess such riches. Formerly she had thought of people living in wooden houses with five rooms as millionaires, to be deferred to in speech and manners. But when she saw Khun Nai's mansion, those wooden houses seemed no different from her own tumbledown, lean-to shack. The rich people she had known seemed to her now like poor, undignified country hicks because, as well as owning so much land that she had to collect the rent herself, Khun Nai was in the pawned goods business. Phanni, who served her closely, became accustomed to seeing vast amounts of gold, silver and valuables each day.

Phanni's life was divided into two distinct parts: from birth to age nine, and from nine to fourteen. She had been born into poverty, and surrounded by it from the beginning. Everything she saw during that time signified deprivation, so that poverty became her natural condition rather than something out of the ordinary. She had no desire for better-ment, because she had no opportunity for close observation of anything better.

Her life changed when she came to live with Khun Nai. When Khun Nai agreed to buy Phanni from her mother, she had said she would buy her as a daughter. The words still resounded in Phanni's ears, but that was the first and last time that she heard them, for as soon as her mother had gone she knew that she was now a slave.

No chore was too low or too heavy for Phanni, in Khun Nai's eyes. No punishment was too great for the slightest misdemeanour. The feeling of poverty dogged her like a shadow she could not throw off. She realized that she was better fed so that she could keep up her strength for work. Her sarongs and blouses were no longer in tatters, but she guessed that this was only because Khun Nai was ashamed of having a servant dressed in rags like a pauper. She was as poor now as she had ever been, with the major difference that now she was poor in the midst of plenty—a poor person sitting in the midst of vast piles of gold and silver, surrounded by tantalizing temptations which created an overwhelming desire for possession. Before, she had lived in abject poverty, with nothing except an empty stomach, the viscissitudes of the climate, and physical fatigue to drive home the feeling that poverty meant suffering. But Khun Nai's valuable possessions, which Phanni saw at close quarters every day, created a hunger that food could not satisfy; a heat that would not be quenched by water or cooled by wind; and an ache that would not respond to ointment or massage, in the depth of the heart itself. During this time, poverty was like an instrument of torture for Phanni. Everything she saw fanned the flame of her desire in a way she had never experienced before. All she could do was sit and look, and think to herself, "One day I'll have things like this. I must have things like this!"

Khun Nai was single and childless, as she had said. But she had raised a nephew and niece. The boy, Phong, was about two years older than Phanni, and his younger sister Philaiphan (Philai for short) was about her age. Phanni called them both *khun*,[*] but like all children of the same age living in the same

[*] A polite term used to address people in general. In this context it is used to address a person with higher status.

house, they used to play together despite the differences in status. Phanni knew that the other two were her superiors, and Philai was quick to remind her if ever she forgot the fact. Phong was a quiet, unassuming fellow. He was kind to Phanni, because she was both younger and a girl, and always shared his sweets with her and did not put on airs. Naturally she preferred him to Philai.

Phanni's feelings towards Phong changed gradually, as he reached maturity. When he was about fifteen his voice began to break, his body expanded, his limbs grew long and robust. She would look at him as he walked, and listen to his deep voice as he talked and laughed. Phanni, aged thirteen, decided he was attractive.

At first, she only went as far as thinking Phong was attractive. Then she heard some of the older servants saying, "Whoever gets a man like Master Phong for a husband will be in luck. Good looking, kind, and rich to boot. If anything happens to Khun Nai, Phong'll inherit," and her feelings began to change. Naively, she thought that getting to be Phong's wife would be a step towards possession of the wealth she hankered after. It seemed an easy route, and one well worth trying, especially as she thought he was handsome. In fact she had not yet experienced any sexual feeling or desire, but as she mixed with adults who did not believe in hiding the details of sexual relations from children, she was well aware of what being husband and wife meant in physical terms. She followed this up by speculating that if she could seduce Phong into doing that with her, she would automatically move up to being his wife. Her deprivation would come to an end, and anything she wanted would drift her way.

With these simple thoughts, Phanni began to flirt with Phong. She smiled at him and gave him meaningful looks, and hurried diligently to act on his every wish. She began to feel that he was taking more notice of her. Sometimes if she were sitting alone he would secretly stare at her, but if she returned his gaze he would quickly turn away. His behaviour satisfied Phanni that her efforts were meeting with success. One day, as she was taking a bath at the back of the house, a sarong wrapped around her breasts, she caught a glimpse of Phong gazing at her from one of the upstairs windows. She pretended not to have noticed him and continued calmly with her bath, in a manner she calculated to be particularly appealing.

Phanni conducted herself in this way for two months, by which time she was sure of success. Phong's way of speaking to her had changed markedly, and his eyes had a hidden gleam she had not seen before. Every night after Khun Nai and her nephew and niece had retired for the night it was Phanni's duty to shut the doors and windows and put up an old mosquito net for herself under the stairs. She was supposed to act as a watch-keeper, even during her sleeping hours.

One night she awoke, startled, at the touch of a hand. Just as she was about to scream, Phong stepped inside the mosquito net and put his hand over her mouth as a signal to keep quiet, while whispering in her ear, "It's only me, Roen, don't make a fuss."

Phanni lay still, not moving a muscle. Buoyant and satisfied, she smiled to herself in the dark. Phong sat close to her. The hand across her mouth moved to feel and caress her face, ears, and neck, and finally her breasts, hesitant, as if not quite sure what to do. Phanni did not object or resist. A smile played around her lips, as her heart beat faster. His hand reached lower, trembling with excitement. It was totally dark, and they could not see each other, but Phong's hand found its way all over Phanni's body, in excitement and curiosity. It was the first time Phong had been so close to someone of the opposite sex. He knew that his desire was growing stronger. His hands burned hotly. A moment later he lay down beside her, slowly and carefully. He turned to face Phanni, who lay in her original pose, on her back. He threw his arm and leg over her in an awkward and inexpert way, and in that instant he held her tightly. A tremor seemed to pass through him, and his heated breathing resounded in her ear for a few brief seconds. Then suddenly everything changed. The passion subsided. Phong stretched his rigid form, then got up hurriedly without saying a word.

Phanni lay awake under her net for a long time. She did not understand why Phong had left so abruptly. Her high spirits evaporated; the vision of heaps of gold and silver gave way in the darkness to an ordinary old torn mosquito net; the smell of youthful vigour was replaced by the dank smell of the net she had not had time to wash. She thought she must have displeased him in some way, not realizing that Phong, in his youth and his first experience of a woman, had reached the peak of his gratification and had retreated in embarrassment, intending to return another night. He did not know that his sister Philai, under the net adjacent to him, was not asleep. When Phong crept downstairs, she had followed him to the foot of the staircase. Peering over, she knew where he had gone, and stored it up to report to her aunt the next morning.

Phanni had never imagined that anyone could be as angry as Khun Nai was when she scolded her. Late the next morning Khun Nai vented her unrestrained anger, verbally and physically. Phong was sent away from the house immediately. Khun Nai came up to Phanni, grabbed her by the head, took off the slippers she wore round the house, and beat her mercilessly. At the same time she abused her, with a vocabulary such as Phanni had never dreamed of from such a well-bred lady. Khun Nai bashed her and shouted at her until she went numb. She did not attempt to resist or escape because she knew that she would not get far. Khun Nai, exhausted by blows and curses, finally raised her foot and kicked Phanni with such force that she was flung from the porch, down a flight of steps, onto the lower landing. Khun Nai then turned and went inside, and kept cursing all afternoon. At no point did she utter a word to banish Phanni. Attachment to the fifty baht she had invested in her was an even greater tie for Khun Nai than it was for Phanni herself.

An elderly lady, *Yai** Khlip, used to set up a stall selling grilled bananas every day out in front of Phanni's house. Phanni knew her well, because these bananas were all she could afford with the pittance Khun Nai occasionally threw in her direction. Whenever she was upset, or anxious about something, she went out and bought Yai Khlip's bananas to nibble on. The day after the incident she did not dare appear before Khun Nai, but stayed in the kitchen, out of the way. As soon as Yai Khlip set up her stand Phanni sneaked out of the house to buy some bananas to console herself. Seeing her swollen cheek and bruised body, Yai Khlip asked, "What's the matter with you dear, your face is all swollen!"

"She slapped me, Auntie," Phanni replied.

"Who slapped you?"

"Khun Nai did, Auntie."

"What had you done?"

"She accused me of seducing her nephew, Auntie."

"Ah!" Yai Khlip flashed a glance at Phanni and asked casually,

* Literally, 'grandma'. It is also used to address any elderly women with lower status.

"And what did you do?"

"I didn't do anything," Phanni excused herself, then continued, head bowed, "He just came and slept with me, and next morning his sister went off and told, so Khun Nai slapped and thrashed me."

"Hmm!" Yai Khlip sighed deeply and said, "Heartless person, thrashing you like that. I feel sorry for you, poor little thing." She stopped turning the bananas grilling on the stove for a minute and said, "Don't stay with her. Come with me. I'll put you into the care of a really kind person, where you'll have beautiful clothes and lots of money. Will you come?"

"I'd like to," Phanni answered, "But I'm scared she'd come after me and get me."

"Don't worry, take my word for it. If she follows you, I'll put the police onto her myself. What a person! Beating you like a cow or a buffalo," Yai Khlip said as she packed her things away in preparation for leaving. "Come with me, I'd like to see you live well. Come on."

"When'll you be going, Auntie?" Phanni asked, half-persuaded, half-suspecting.

"Right now. If we stay for long she'll get suspicious." With these words Yai Khlip lifted her yoke onto her shoulders and set off, the other hand firmly gripping the wrist of Phanni, who followed in bewilderment.

PHANNI followed old Khlip through the streets, lanes and alleyways. The people coming and going did not show any interest or turn to stare. On the way Khlip stopped to buy a new blouse and skirt for her—the first new clothes she had had in her life. At the end of a long alley they finally came to a little house, which Khlip said was her own. She called Phanni in, gave her a bath, found her some food, and showed her more kindness than she had ever before experienced. That evening Khlip announced, "Little Roen, tomorrow I'll take you to stay with a relative of mine in the provinces. If you stay here they might send someone after you and there'd be trouble for nothing. Leave town for a while till it dies down, then I'll come back and get you."

Phanni took Khlip at her word, her behaviour having demonstrated her good intentions. Next morning she took Phanni to the railway staion to catch the morning train to Lop Buri, where she took her to a house well protected by fences, not far from the market.

Inside, Phanni saw a couple of girls wandering around in sarongs and chemises, their hair unkempt as if they had just woken, and their eyes dull from lack of sleep the previous night. Their faces showed traces of powder and rouge incompletely washed away. When Phanni arrived with Khlip, a middle-aged lady came rushing out of her room and greeted Khlip enthusiastically.

"Khian," Khlip said, "I've brought my niece to put in your charge. Look after her—she's only a kid. She's not bad look-ing."

"Sure, no problem," said the lady called Khian, "Any niece of yours is a niece of mine too. Don't you worry, I'll take good care of her."

The girls who had been wandering around came in and sat at a distance. Hearing Khian speak, they giggled. They looked first at Phanni, then at each other, and laughed as if Khian had just said something uproariously funny.

"What's your name?" *Nang* (Mrs.) Khian asked.

"My name is Roen," Phanni answered.

"That's not a very nice name," Nang Khian remarked, "Change it. I'll think of one for you. Now let me see . . . How about this! There used to be a Phanni here, but she's gone now, so how about you become Phanni instead of her. Does it sound nice?"

"Yes, it does."

"Remember your name then," Nang Khian admonished her, and from then on Roen used the name Phanni as her pseudonym in her profession.

Nang Khian showed Phanni into a room with a cupboard, bed, and full range of toiletries, and told her that this was to be her own room. She told her to make herself completely at home, and to let her know if she wanted for anything, because she was very fond of children. Then she left her alone in the room. Phanni considered herself very fortunate to have met such a kind person.

In the afternoon, when Khlip had returned to Bangkok, Nang Khian was extremely attentive to Phanni. She took her to the dressmaker, and to buy accessories, and bought her many different kinds of cosmetics. That evening she took her to have her hair permed. It seemed that there was nothing Nang Khian would not give her, and Phanni could only be amazed at her good fortune. The heavy weight of poverty already seemed to be lifting, and the world seemed a better place. When she got home Phanni noticed a few men sitting talking to the same girls she had seen that morning. The men turned and looked at her with interest, but Nang Khian hurried her through to her room and told her to have a good sleep. Next morning they would have a chat about things. She instructed her not to come out of her room on any account, and not to take any notice of the men outside.

"They're all members of my family," she explained, and left the room, imprisoning Phanni inside.

Phanni dozed fitfully until late, puzzled by the frequent

nocturnal comings and goings in the house. Through the darkness she could hear the sounds of people going up and down stairs, laughing and talking, doors opening and shutting, and the continuous sound of running water from people going to the bathroom in the backyard.

Nang Khian was so pleasant during her first four or five days in the house that Phanni thought she was the kindest person she had ever known. On the fifth or sixth day Nang Khian called Phanni over and said, "Did you know that someone is in love with you, dearie?"

"Who is it, auntie?" Phanni asked, not knowing what to say.

"The Chinese man who runs the gold shop," Nang Khian answered. "He really loves you. Tonight I'll let him have a chat with you in your room. He's got lots of money. If you do what he wants and look after him well, he'll give us lots of money. I'll give some of it to you to spend, and keep some to buy things for you. Make sure you humour him, won't you. Don't be afraid, he really does love you, he told me so himself. If I didn't think he did I wouldn't let him come and chat."

"But I wouldn't know what to say to him—I don't even know him! I'll be so embarrassed!" Phanni said awkwardly. Inwardly she was beginning to feel obligated to Nang Khian.

"Heavens! That doesn't matter!" Nang Khian exclaimed. "The old Chinaman is very kind. You'll soon get to know him, and you're sure to like him, too."

Phanni could not think what else to say, so remained silent. That night she was prey to a heated, destructive, cruel lust; to a desire by which men forget their humanity and behave like dumb beasts. She could not escape, or even struggle against the big, strong man who entered her room that night.

Her pain on that first occasion was emotional as well as physical. She came to regard sex as having no meaning other than money, a financial return. After the events of that night Phanni clearly understood her own position, that of Nang Khian, the house she lived in, and its other inhabitants. She found out that old Khlip had sold her to Nang Khian for three hundred baht. She had to 'work' to pay that back, but she could not calculate how many hundreds of years it would take to repay the debt. For every moment that she spent in the house, all items of expenditure—clothes, face powder, electricity, cooking charcoal, every drop of water and every grain of rice—seemed to be added to the original three hundred baht Nang Khian had paid out. Nevertheless, either because Nang Khian had some residual kindness or because she wanted to placate Phanni, who was burgeoning into a fruitful source of income, she always gave her enough for her personal use. This was the first time Phanni had had money of her own to spend, and even though it was not much, it was real money. She had earned it through her own sacrifice and endurance in the first instance, although later it became habitual and occasionally even enjoyable, when it was not tiring or painful. Had the first man who bought satisfaction from Phanni been ugly or repulsive she might have dreaded the life awaiting her, but Nang Khian was shrewd and experienced enough to have arranged a young Chinese, who all the residents agreed was 'handsome'. The good looks of this first man helped mitigate the agony of that night: the absence of physically repugnant qualities concealed and obscured the emotional revulsion.

Nang Khian used Phanni sparingly, and did not have her come out and receive guests as the others did. Those who wanted to 'chat' with Phanni in her room would have to make a special arrangement, for a high price, with Nang Khian. She made sure that neither their looks nor their age would be too off-putting, so that "the kid wouldn't take fright," and explained that "for new ones it's best to give them who they like, then once they're used to it they can take anybody."

If a child's body is stimulated by adult actions and emotions, it will rapidly reach a physical maturity beyond its age, and emotional development will follow. Phanni matured physically and mentally according to this rule and she became a woman at an early age. Earning her living by satisfying the sexual desire of others made her interested in, and eager for, men. After a while she asked whether she, too, could receive guests every night. It gave her a chance to earn more, and she could no longer bear to stay in her room alone when she could hear the sound of voices and other activities going on in the rooms around her. When Phanni put her request, Nang Khian obliged, and from then on the word got around that Nang Khian's establishment had 'a new one'.

But Phanni's stay in Lop Buri was to be short-lived because it so happened that one night the police raided the brothel, rounded up Nang Khian and all the other inhabitants, and took them to the police station. A policeman kindly disposed towards his fellows took pity on Phanni on account of her youth and childlike air and released her from Nang Khian, sending her on her way with the fare to Bangkok. When questioned, she had told him she had come from there, but had been deceived and sold into prostitution. Her face bathed in tears, she had claimed that it had been entirely against her will and that her foremost wish was to go home.

She boarded the train in high spirits. Now she was her own boss, free to do as she pleased. Before she left, friends in the house had whispered the name and address of a hotel in Bangkok to her. She would use that as her base for earning her living. She felt secure in the knowledge that she was still young and healthy, with plenty of time ahead to earn easy money.

At the same time, she looked forward to keeping her entire earnings for herself. A rosy future beckoned her, giving no cause for worry.

Phanni reached the hotel safely and embarked on the only profession she knew. She had not reckoned with the strange properties of money: it did not stay still, and the more one earned, the more ways of spending it there seemed to be. Sometimes she felt like a millionaire, and spent freely, learning the ropes of gambling on anything from races to cards. At other times she felt as poor and deprived as ever, because she had no obligations to restrict her expenditure. Being alone in the world, without ties, was both a blessing and a burden.

Nor had Phanni taken into account the laws of nature, which manifest themselves in unlikely situations at inconvenient times. Unwittingly, she fell pregnant. By the time she realized, it was too late to do anything about it. When she knew for certain that she was pregnant she felt a sense of panic that she would lose her attractiveness, as well as valuable working time. Her friends told her of an abortifacient, and she went along with them, in a daze, and actually purchased the medicine. Yet when the time came, she could not bring herself to take it. Her own past experience had taught her, involuntarily, that life was precious and not to be easily destroyed. On the contrary, it was something to be maintained at all costs. The baby in her womb represented a new life, and no matter how she had been accustomed to conduct herself, she still believed that it was a grave sin to destroy a living creature.

As the time of the birth approached Phanni began to look around for a place to have the child, and to put money aside for the purpose. Her thoughts turned to home, to her own mother, and she decided that the most suitable arrangement would be to have the baby at her mother's and leave it for her mother to look after. When she was earning again she would remit a portion to her mother, to support both her own baby and her mother too. Phanni travelled home from Bangkok, and told old Riu everything. Riu acquiesced in all Phanni's conditions. Aging, she no longer had the strength for heavy labour. Regular money from her daughter would improve her position con-siderably. Riu never asked who the child's father was. She knew that Phanni would not know the answer, just as she had never been able to say who Phanni's father was.

After the birth of her child Phanni's empty heart filled with love and affection. Her love for her son seemed greater than that of most other people because she had never experienced it before. At first she thought she would hurry back to Bangkok, but her love for her child was like a weight which would not allow her to slip easily away. The money she had brought with her was running low. She knew she would have to head back to Bangkok to start earning again, but it was hard for her to leave behind her baby, so recently born. Yet to take him would hinder Phanni's livelihood, and could force her to re-encounter a state of poverty to which she never wanted to return. After long hesitation she decided, tears streaming down her face, to return to Bangkok. She resolved that her child should never undergo such poverty as had once been hers. She would do everything in her power to better her child's position, no matter what the difficulties or sacrifices.

Phanni's figure had become fuller and more attractive following childbirth and she pursued her profession more zealously. She no longer pursued the dictates of her emotions. Once she had lived for her own pleasure: if she did not like a man's looks or manner she would not go with him, no matter how much he offered—and if she liked a man, she would satisfy him for nothing, taking their mutual pleasure as her reward.

Now, however, her object was to earn as much as possible. Spurred on by her love and hopes for her child, she went with anyone who had money. Sometimes her eagerness for a fast buck led her along the wrong path. She gambled more than ever. At times, gambling seemed to bring the celestial mansions before her very gaze, and at others she lay breaking into a sweat, her hands covering her face at visions of the poverty that lay in wait.

Phanni's overwhelming desire for money made her dissatisfied with her irregular income. She set out to look for somewhere she could make a lot of money on a permanent basis. Some of her friends were learning to dance, to frequent the dance halls at night, and eventually well-off Thais or foreigners took them off and kept them. She knew what men were like, and that she could take them for a complete ride if she only had the chance to get near them. So she decided to learn to dance. Within a short time she danced well. Following an initial investment in two or three modern evening dresses, Phanni became a regular nightly fixture at the dance hall.

The dance hall enhanced Phanni's awareness of a wider world. She had only known men who met her in secret, who would have been too embarrassed to acknowledge or greet her if they ran into her elsewhere. She had formerly existed on the fringes of society, in a twilight zone, but her new life exposed her to the world. The foreigners who came to relax were not bound by restrictions or responsibilities. As they were merely passing through on their way to their homes, their leisure behaviour evaded the restraints of shame. Pleasure was their object, and they made no attempt to hide the fact. Thus, the atmosphere there differed from other places, and affected the Thais who went there too.

Phanni's income rose because she cultivated foreigners, who

had more money to throw around, rather than Thais. She experienced much that was new through associating with foreigners. Her behaviour, down to her dress and makeup, became more stylish. From an ageing prostitute, she turned into a fresh socialite. Poverty, and being a slave to other people's money, seemed a long way off, and at times the spectre almost faded away altogether. Through mixing with foreigners, Phanni picked up their language, with the agility of one who has never undergone formal training. She had no preconceptions about the importance of language, so she did not let complex grammar or vocabulary hamper the free expression of her thoughts or feelings in a foreign tongue. To her, English was just another of the world's many languages, and with only a few words of it she could make herself clearly understood to her foreign friends. Her every sentence would alarm anyone who had studied the language, yet all the foreigners understood. These sentences were, "You go *kon si* (before)! *Laeo* (then) I *cha* (will) follow," or "I sleep with you—for three hundred *tic*—all night," and "No! No! I not go for two hundred but for two hundred fifty I go!" or "Tomorrow you come again *na* (okay)?"

Perhaps it was her pleasing appearance, perhaps her easy-going nature. Whatever the reason, the foreigners she met liked her. Some came back after spending a night with her, and returned as often as they could until they finally left Thailand. Others took such a liking to her they jealously set her up in their own houses. She always agreed instantly, and asked for exorbitant amounts of money and expensive goods during their time together. When she could no longer ask for more, she walked out, or, if her 'game' was exposed, was kicked out. She left without regret or resentment, because she saw no distinct-ion between leaving voluntarily and being expelled. The person she had broken off with had either run out of money to keep her or decided not to give her any. She had no desire for relations with men who could not reward her financially.

DURING her four or five years in the dance hall and in various houses, Phanni visited her child at every opportunity. She got tens of thousands, and although most of it went in gambling and pandering to her own appearance, which she considered as a professional investment, she never forgot to send some home. Riu was able to use the money to build a new house, and to buy a plot of land to rent out for income to keep her and her grandchild. Phanni's child grew up cheerful and talkative, giving her happiness such as she had never known before. The more pleasure he gave her, the more determined she was to earn even more to make him happy.

One day, as she was sitting in the dance hall, a young man came over and asked her to dance. She was taken aback with shock when she saw his face. She recognized Phong instantly. At first she thought he had not remembered her, after so long, but when she rose to dance with him he said, "Roen! Imagine seeing you! What are you doing here? You've turned into quite a beauty!"

That night Phanni lay smiling in the darkness of a hotel room. Phong slept beside her. Earlier in the evening he had told her his story. After Phanni left he had returned to live at Khun Nai's, and a while later she sent him to study abroad. He returned to Thailand after a three- or four-year 'immersion' overseas. Khun Nai died four or five months after his return, leaving him her entire fortune. Phong was now an eminently eligible young man, in looks, nature, and wealth. The third feature was particularly to Phanni's liking. She knew that she was getting on, and that if she could manage to get someone like him to support her, she would solve the problem of age and reduced earnings. Phanni knew the extent of Phong's wealth. If he were to support her, then her child would be well provided for too. She did not give a thought to Phong himself. He was a symbol of past oppression, and she would happily see him impoverished on her account.

That night, Phanni knew that Phong desired her. Last time, he had been thwarted. Meeting her again, those same constraints incited insatiable desires. While she entertained him with her body, she began to bind him to her emotionally, by relating her story. Playing for sympathy, she told him that after he was sent away she had been beaten and ill-treated so by Khun Nai that she had had to escape. On her own, she had experienced bitter hardship and been forced to do heavy work as a labourer. At this point she remembered to hint that all her trials and tribulations were Phong's fault. Finally, she told him, she married a poor labourer, but he died after she had given birth to their first child. The burden of providing for the child had brought her to work in the dance halls. She stressed repeatedly, until Phong was convinced, that she only danced with her clients, that was all. After work she went straight home, and did not conduct herself in the loose fashion that most people seemed to expect. She was sleeping with Phong, that night, out of love. Her tears and her whole demeanour led Phong to believe most of the fictional tale she had concocted. Next morning, when they parted, he was convinced she was telling the truth because she absolutely refused to accept a cent in payment.

From then on Phong was a regular visitor. With the hundred and one wiles of a prostitute, Phanni tightened the noose around him until he could move no more. He thought nothing was too expensive for her; no sum of money she asked for was too great, and eventually he was pleading with her repeatedly

to come and live with him as his wife. She
offhand way, saying that she did not want her lo
to damage his standing. Her refusals egged him on, an
she agreed, he promised excitedly to have the marriage lega
registered.

Phanni asked Phong's permission to return home to visit her
child. He granted it willingly. When she mentioned that she
would also like thirty thousand baht to build a house, he gave
it unstintingly.

Once home, she handed the money over to her mother, and
frankly related the whole Phong saga. Old Riu said, "Believe
me, Roen, don't go back to Bangkok. Stay here, with your
mother and child. We've got enough money now. Don't go
back to work on him, it's not right. I don't know what it was
we did in our past lives, but I think we've paid for it now!"

Phanni listened, and laughed, unperturbed. Merit and fate
were old people's talk: she had no time for such things. Had
she been worried about them from the outset, she and her
mother might still be slaving away in the name of fate.

AS the boat headed for Bangkok that night, Phanni sat with
her eyes shut, thinking about the glowing future ahead. She
would be fantastically wealthy. If the edge of her blouse had
not caught on the door of the engine room when the boat
over-turned, she might have escaped death.

That morning her corpse lay on the bank, alone and
unadorned. Before anyone had thought to find an old sack to
cover her, four or five country youths crowded around. Some
of them flushed with desire, others nudged each other and
sniggered. Even after she had breathed her last, Phanni's body
still aroused lust, and was still public property.

THE PRINCE

PRINCE Lek did not have a grand name like all the other princes because he had been born just after the death of his father, a high-ranking prince, over fifty years ago. His elder brothers and sisters, offspring of his father's many wives, were all named appropriately, in rhyming sequence. Prince Lek's mother was the youngest wife, and his father had died when she was a little more than eight months pregnant. When Prince Lek was born, no-one was interested in giving him a proper name. No-one even bothered to register the birth of the new prince with the Palace Ministry. Everyone in the palace therefore called him simply 'Prince Lek', 'the little prince'. His mother was too young to think of calling him anything else. Even though he was born a prince, his royalty was only a matter of his own perception and that of the general populace. No-one had registered his birth, he was not officially regarded as a prince, and was not paid an annual stipend like other royalty. However, no-one stopped him from using the title 'Prince' Lek, nor did anyone object when he entered the palace for the annual blessing with lustral water by the King.

Since Prince Lek had never seen his father, his image of him was formed from the two or three old photographs which hung in the former residence, and the little photograph that his mother had hanging in her house. Whenever he thought of his father, the source of his royal blood, he never thought of the face in those photographs, but harked back instead to other objects associated with him in his memory. His father's body had been kept for many years in an upper hall, in the residence that people in the palace called the throne hall, and had still not been cremated when Prince Lek had grown old enough to remember. Hence every time he thought of his father, he recalled the urn set on a high raised platform in the closed, darkened throne hall. It was not a pleasant memory. He vividly remembered that the throne hall which housed the urn was dark and stuffy because it had been closed for so long. Cobwebs had settled on the windows, on the intricate carving of the urn's platform, and on the ceremonial umbrellas surrounding it. As his father's body was shut away, no-one had paid it much attention. Prince Lek remembered that his mother had taken him to prostrate himself in obeisance to the urn, and pointed out to him that his father was in there. He had thought, as a child of four or five would, that his father had always lived in there, and marvelled at how he had managed to keep so still.

A year later Prince Lek was to understand with finality that the father in the urn had been dead for a long time. He remembered that the palace residents suddenly began to show unusual signs of activity. His mother prepared white clothes for herself and her son, and whispered that his father was to be given a royal cremation. When he asked whether his father would not feel terribly hot, she cried and told him that his father had been dead in the urn for many years and that by now there would probably be barely anything of him left.

One day, a number of men dressed in blue silk draped trousers, white jackets, and mourning armbands, with maroon badges at their collars, came to the palace and went straight to the throne hall where the urn was kept. Prince Lek entered with his mother. Many of his sisters and brothers, and his other 'mothers', were already seated. Some were crying, some sitting chatting, but his mother cried more than anyone. The other wives turned around and stared, and the eldest child scolded her. The officiants spread a white cloth in the middle of the room and then went up to remove the outer layer of the urn. Instead of his father, Prince Lek saw an inner lining of dull gold, which was 'invited' to descend. When this was opened, one of the officiants raised his hands in salutation and reached down to pick up an object, the shape and colour of a decayed coconut husk, to place in the middle of the cloth. Prince Lek learnt later that the object was his father's head. Other dried up sections of his body followed. His clothes were removed and part of the body covered with a white cloth. Each of his sisters and brothers crawled over to sprinkle the objects laid out on the white cloth. Eventually his mother nudged him and handed him a small bottle of perfume, and whispered to him to bathe his father for the last time. In fact it was both the first and last time, but he could not bring himself to believe that the stuffy shrivelled remains he saw in front of him were those of his father, his progenitor.

Over the next four or five days, the atmosphere in the palace was livelier than Prince Lek had ever known it. People came and went, day and night. Another group of people, dressed in red coats and trousers, set themselves up in the pavilion next to the main palace and played flutes and beat drums at intervals. His mother said they were proclaiming his father's death. But he did not understand why she had to cry every time the flutes and drums sounded out. He was too young to realize that music can cause sorrow as well as happiness.

After the cremation, Prince Lek noticed the chaos around him. Most of the people who had lived in the palace began to disappear one by one, or family by family, until no-one was left. One day his mother packed up everything in the house she had always lived in and which he had always regarded as his home. When he asked her about it, she explained that they could not stay on any longer, because during his lifetime his father had borrowed heavily from the royal treasury to support the palace staff necessary to maintain his status as a senior prince. No-one had been able to repay his debts after his death, and therefore the palace had reverted to the royal treasury. All his elder siblings had had to move elsewhere, and as for Prince Lek, his mother would take him to live with his grandmother.

HIS grandmother had an old wooden house in the traditional style, built on land rented from the temple. She was very old, and a young girl who was a distant relative stayed with her. When Prince Lek and his mother came to stay, it made four. Prince Lek had the old house to eat and sleep in, and the temple grounds to play in. In time, he was placed in the temple school. Every time the teacher referred to him as 'His Serene Highness Prince Lek', the other children would turn and stare and snigger, as if he were some strange object that had landed in the school. Precisely because the teacher called him 'His Serene Highness Prince Lek', his avenues for making friends with any of the other children were blocked by a wall. The obstacle was his royal birth, which prevented his classmates from getting as close to him as they would to a fellow commoner. Because the teacher always used royal language in addressing Prince Lek, the other children felt awkward and did not know how they should speak to him. Thus he was kept apart, a freak to be pointed out and avoided the whole time he was at school.

About a year after they moved, Prince Lek noticed that a man about his mother's age was a frequent visitor to the house. She always smiled and laughed when he came, and sometimes they sat and talked together for long periods. His mother explained that he was a relative, like a cousin, whom he must address as 'uncle'. Every time Uncle came to the house, he used to bring something for his mother and sweets for Prince Lek. He got to know this uncle and looked forward to his visits because he saw that they cheered his mother up so, but his mother's behaviour had begun to change so markedly he could not help noticing. Some days she would sit gazing in front of her, sighing deeply. At other times she sat alone, crying, and even when Prince Lek tried to ask her what the matter was, she refused to tell him.

One day Uncle came to the house to see his mother and they sat talking for a long time. Prince Lek noticed that his mother was crying as she spoke, and that however much Uncle tried to console her, he was unsuccessful. Eventually Uncle got up and took his leave, and when Prince Lek ran to say goodbye at the head of the stairs, Uncle gathered him up close and whispered to him to behave and to do well so that he could support his mother, because when Uncle went away this time, he would not be coming back.

That night his mother put Prince Lek to bed first, but she stayed up, with the lamp lit, outside the mosquito net. Prince Lek lay awake, staring at the mosquito net ceiling. He could hear her crying to herself as if she harboured a deep sorrow. Lying still, he felt sorry for her, but did not know how to comfort or help her. He had already noticed that whenever she cried and was sad, things seemed only to become worse if he went to her, and she cried more than ever. Moments later he heard his grandmother enter. After the sound of murmured speech, his mother sobbed a bit louder, then his grandmother said, "I don't see the problem. If you really love Bunsom, agree to his proposal to live together as man and wife. I don't see how anyone could object to that."

Prince Lek began to listen to the conversation outside the net more intently, as Bunsom was Uncle's name, and this was the first time he had known that his mother loved Uncle Bunsom. His mother responded, between sobs, "No, Mother . . . I can't . . . I really couldn't. For the rest of this life I'll live to raise my son as I am now, but I'll never take another husband."

"I just don't understand," his grandmother said. "If you marry Bunsom he can support you and your child. You'll be better off, with enough to eat and spend. If you weren't in love I wouldn't say all this, but you told me you loved him."

"I have never loved anyone more in my whole life," his mother said, "but I had to decide to tell him never to see me again. On my own, without a child, it'd be reasonable, or even if my child were a commoner I would've consented . . . but I have a child . . . a royal child . . . I have to preserve myself so that my son won't grow up to be ashamed of me. Don't forget, my child is a prince." She burst into tears again, while his grandmother remained silent, and sighed deeply.

Prince Lek lay perfectly still, his eyes wide open. He did not dare move for fear that his mother would know he was not asleep yet. His cheeks were wet with tears. For the first time, he realized how much his mother loved him, enough for her to sacrifice her own happiness, even her own life, for his. He began to feel that he was an obstacle to the happiness of the one he loved, his mother, the only support he had left in the world. Prince Lek knew that he was just a boy like any other, but the rank that had propped him up from birth loomed over him like a massive and fearsome shadow. It intervened to prevent him from getting close to the other pupils at school, and now it was a barrier preventing his mother, whom he loved more than anyone, from realizing happiness in her life. The rank which differentiated him from others began to feel to him like a wound. Only a small scratch now, it showed signs of spreading, and could eventually be crippling.

FROM that day on, no-one at home ever spoke of uncle Bunsom, and, as he had promised, he did not reappear. His mother never cried in front of him again, but Prince Lek knew from her face that she despaired of life and had lost interest in her physical well-being. She rarely smiled or laughed, and when occasionally she did smile at Prince Lek, it was merely to conceal her inner suffering and deep despair.

His mother and grandmother made sweets, and got one of the young granddaughters to sell them. This continued for some time, until his mother became thin and fell ill, hardly able to work any more. Eventually, she could not get up at all and was confined to bed. His grandmother, who was already very old, had to work harder than ever at making sweets for a living as well as caring for her ailing daughter. The problem of earning a living became crucial when one day, the young granddaughter ran away from home. No-one could find her, and after a number of days she still had not returned

"Well, what are we going to do now?" grandmother remarked one day as she sat hugging her knees alongside her daughter's bed, with Prince Lek beside her.

"When Waen was here, she helped go about selling the sweets," she continued, "but now she's gone, who's going to sell sweets if I make them? I'll have to sell them as well as make them, and how am I going to get the strength for that, at my age? But I'll have to, or else we'll starve, the lot of us."

His mother looked away quickly, hiding her face in the

pillow, and lay sobbing. Her mother comforted her, saying, "Don't be unhappy, child. You just make sure you get well and truly better soon, so you can help me earn a living." She sighed, and dragged her bent old body off to make more sweets.

After his grandmother had left, his mother still lay crying quietly, not having the will or energy to move to do any- thing else. Prince Lek edged closer to her on the mattress and said softly, "Mummy, Mummy, please don't cry. You don't have to worry about anything. I'm big enough now, I'll go out and sell the sweets for Grandmother."

His mother started in shock as if something had struck her violently, and lifted her arm, wasted and skinny from fever, to draw him close to her bosom. Through her sobs, she said in a trembling voice, "My darling prince, don't say such things! I'd rather die. You're a prince . . . you can't go out and sell sweets like an ordinary boy. I'd starve rather than have you do that. On no account do that . . . you can't." She hugged him tightly, sobbing as though her heart would indeed break.

From that day on, Prince Lek could only sit and watch his mother become increasingly ill and emaciated, and see creeping poverty and deprivation overtake his family. His mother had to sell off her few remaining possessions, one by one, to get enough money to keep the family alive from day to day. Prince Lek wanted to alleviate the sufferings of his mother and grandmother by devoting all his physical energy to their well-being, but he was unable to do so because his mother could not forget that her son was of royal blood. Because of this, any heavy physical labour he was able to do, as he was already twelve years old, such as lifting and carrying, was completely forbidden him. His royal lineage became a prison whereby he observed the suffering that went on around him without being able in the slightest degree to get rid of the wretchedness.

And because he knew himself to have been incarcerated and handicapped by his birth, he experienced the suffering a thousandfold. Sometimes he woke in the middle of the night, startled and bathed in sweat, as if he had woken from a nightmare. He would lie thinking of the hardships ahead of him as a massive wall which he had no chance of scaling, and when he heard his mother cough or moan softly from her sickbed, he could only cry alone, trying to swallow his sobs for fear she would hear him.

Suffering and poverty exacerbate disease. His mother's condition would not go away, but deteriorated as time went on. She became just skin and bone, and burst into tears whenever she saw Prince Lek. She received no treatment because there was no way they could call a doctor. The medicines her mother gave her were all folk remedies, which gave no relief in a serious illness. As Prince Lek watched his mother getting worse, his hopes and dreams dwindled as her life seemed to ebb from her body with every passing day.

But one day Uncle Bunsom appeared on a visit, totally unexpectedly. He had been doing business upcountry for a while, and must have had a premonition on his return, for when he came to Bangkok he dropped by to see Prince Lek's mother. Finding her dangerously ill, he came every day, and brought a doctor in to treat her, but it was too late. Prince Lek sobbed inwardly at the doctor's comment that, "If you'd called me four or five months ago she probably could have been cured, but there's nothing I can do now." He knew that had he not been born a prince he could have helped work for his grandmother and earned enough money to call a doctor before it was too late. His birth was the obstacle which prevented him from saving the life of the mother who had given him birth. She died three or four days later, but as she was gasping for breath she managed to say to Uncle Bunsom, "Som, Som, take care of the prince. He's still so young... and Mother's so old now... please look after him well, for my sake. I... "

She died before completing the sentence, leaving Prince Lek to sit weeping, all alone, feeling that there was nothing else left in the world.

His mother's cremation took place with Uncle Bunsom's support, and Prince Lek was given the opportunity of another four years of schooling. After this, his grandmother also died, and Uncle Bunsom took Prince Lek, now a youth who looked older than his years, to live with him. He entrusted him to friends who arranged for him to enter government service as a clerk, on a monthly salary of fifteen baht. To Prince Lek this seemed a handsome sum, more than he would be able to spend. Because Uncle Bunsom was only a small trader and not a rich man, he paid him eight baht a month for board. Before he accepted the government position he had mentioned the possibility of lending a hand in Uncle Bunsom's business, but his uncle shared his mother's views, and answered, "No, Your Highness, you can't. A prince can't run around trading, it would be dishonourable. People could look down on you, and it would be unpropitious for me, too. Don't do anything else. Government service is best. You'll get to high places in future, befitting your royal birth, and then I'll be able to depend on you when I'm old."

He had heard the reasons Uncle Bunsom gave many times before, from his mother, so many times that they had become part of his nature, accepted as sufficient explanation for all the prohibitions on his activities. Born royal, he could not act like a commoner, yet he lacked the means to act like other royalty he had seen. In the end there was very little he could do. He lived his life within the framework of other people's beliefs and feelings. His own ideas and wishes were unable to destroy those boundaries.

PRINCE Lek experienced love for the first and only time in his life at the age of about twenty. Working at the Ministry, he had to walk from home past the junction, and every evening he returned the same way. There was a shophouse just near the junction, where a flawlessly complexioned girl sat regularly selling betel nut, cigarettes, and assorted dry goods. Whenever he passed the shop he would sneak a glance at her, in the manner of a young man who cannot help looking at a beautiful woman.

In the beginning he did not take much interest, and paid her no more than usual regard in passing, but after some time, passing the shop and seeing the girl became a regular part of his life. If ever he was unable to do so, he felt as though something were missing. The girl's face became part of his consciousness, and he found she often occupied his thoughts. In dreams, she was frequently the important element in the young man's awakening. At a later stage, she began to return his interest, and every time he passed the shop their eyes would meet. Within a short time, the looks became more meaningful.

One day Prince Lek plucked up all his courage, and stopped to buy a packet of cigarettes at the shop. He did not leave immediately after his purchase, but stayed on and drew the girl into conversation on the weather. She was not unwilling, and even seemed pleased that he had dropped by, after having only looked for so long. Prince Lek learnt from their conversation that day that her name was Thawin, and that she was the daughter of the shopowners, who were still living. When she in turn asked him, he said his name was 'Lek'. He did not tell her that he was a prince.

They were soon very close. Thawin's parents, *Nai* (Mr.) Rot and Nang Phat, welcomed him, and permitted him to visit their daughter as he wished. Nobody knew that he was a prince, only that his name was Lek and that he worked as a clerk. This was sufficient and satisfactory for everyone. It was the first time Prince Lek had developed a close and informal relationship with his fellow human beings.

When he got to the shop late in the afternoon, if Nai Rot was at home he would invite Lek to join him for a whisky and a meal. His wife and daughter looked after them. Nai Rot's informal chatter was like rain falling on parched earth to Prince Lek. He did not use the royal language, which is annoying enough when used correctly, and even more grating when misused. He spoke in an easy, unpretentious way, which gained in depth because it came straight from the heart. The comparison with carefully chosen words was like the difference between a real diamond and an imitation. Nai Rot called Prince Lek simply 'Lek' because he did not know who he was. When he saw him in the afternoon he would call out, "There you are, Lek, sit down and have a chat! Make yourself at home, there's no 'us and them' business here!"

Nai Rot would hand him a drink, saying, "Here, have a drink to warm your stomach. Now there, don't worry, we're not going to get drunk or anything. What's the harm? We'll have just enough to give us an appetite."

Then Nai Rot would put the plate of peeled raw mangoes in front of him and continue, "Freshen your mouth with some mango. The kid's mother picked it up at the market today, it's just right." Then he would yell out to the kitchen, "You, Mum! What's for dinner today? Lek's going to join us." Nang Phat's voice would come back with, "Eel soup, ginger beef, and boiled vegetables with chili sauce. It'll be ready in a while. Don't go away now Lek, I've made a whole lot extra just for you."

Moments later the aroma of fried foods, soup and steaming rice would waft through from the kitchen to tantalize those outside. Prince Lek gulped. The harmonious atmosphere within the loving family, their bright, cheerful faces, their speech suffused with love and goodwill, made life in Nai Rot's family seem like heaven, and the food that his wife prepared like ambrosia. The family usually dined together, and sometimes Prince Lek joined the circle. Nai Rot and Nang Phat sensed the young couple's feelings and intentions towards each other from their behaviour, but they did not seem to mind or try to forbid this. The polite, orderly ways he had been trained in were more to their liking than those of other young men who had shown an interest in Thawin.

"YOUNG Lek is strange," Nang Phat reflected aloud one day as they sat chatting. "There's something about him that's different from other youngsters I've seen. It's not just that he's so fair-skinned—I can't think what it is."

Prince Lek was shocked by Nang Phat's remarks, and feared that the conversation would lead on to his origins. Not that he had ever thought to lie or cover up, but when no-one had asked him, he thought it better to suppress the matter first. However, Nai Rot answered for him, "He's a good boy, missus. Anyone who isn't a thug has that air about them. All young men could be like this if they looked out for themselves."

The intimacy and closeness that had built up between them made Prince Lek bold enough to say frankly to Thawin one night, as they sat chatting alone in front of the shop, "Thawin, do you know how much I love you?"

Thawin looked coy and answered softly, "Yes, I do, which is why I'm sitting here talking to you at this hour."

Thawin's answer brought Prince Lek's already brimming happiness to overflowing. He reached out and took her hand, saying awkwardly in a shaky voice, "And do you love me at all, Thawin?"

"I don't know what you're talking about," she replied petulantly in the manner of a young woman. Still, it was not a negative response, and as she did not remove her hand, he took it to be a confession of love. He thought of talking frankly to Thawin and telling her about his background which he had been concealing, but another part of him did not quite dare. He could only say, "Thawin, if I wasn't . . . I wasn't what you thought . . . if I were something else, would you still love me?"

She turned and looked at him for an instant, then said laughingly, "Lek, you really like asking strange questions. You will always be the Lek I see in front of me, how could you be anything else? If you're scared that I'll hold poverty against you then you needn't worry on that score. I don't care whether you're rich or poor, love is a matter of the heart. You needn't be afraid that I'll ever change. All I ask is that you send your elders over to discuss the matter in the customary way. My parents shouldn't stand in our way. They probably won't object and because they're so fond of you they won't ask for much. At most a set of robes for the monks would be enough."

Late that night Prince Lek went home, his heart swelling with happiness and satisfaction. Future happiness seemed to hover within reach. He hoped passionately that another person would share the sorrows and happiness of life with him. He would be lonely no longer. The other would be so intimate as to be like his own self, not allowing any distinction of birth to intervene. On reaching home, he saw Uncle Bunsom sitting in the lamplight. He confessed everything, and begged his uncle to act as his marriage broker, to ask for Thawin's hand, as was the custom. Uncle Bunsom sat thinking for a moment, then said, "Well, that's not a bad idea. It's about time you took a consort and settled down, with someone to look after you. But I'll have to find the auspicious time to ask for her hand. How about this—tomorrow I'll go and have a word with them. If they agree, I'll find out the details of the girl's birthday, and set an auspicious time for both of you."

When he heard Uncle Bunsom talking about a 'consort', Prince Lek started. He had never thought of Thawin as a 'consort', but as a lover, a wife, a lifelong partner. When Uncle Bunsom spoke of a 'consort' it sounded as though Prince Lek was after Thawin to serve and wait on him, which was not what he had in mind at all. A new anxiety gripped him, as he wondered how Thawin and her parents would react to the knowledge that he was a prince. How would Thawin feel when she knew she was going to be a 'consort'!

Next morning Prince Lek left home first thing, to stop off and let Thawin know that his 'elder' was coming to see her that day so that her parents would be home to receive him. For the whole day, as he sat at his desk, his thoughts wandered. He could not predict what the future would bring, but he knew that from that day forward his life would change direction. It could not remain the same, but he could not imagine which way it would go.

That afternoon he hurried straight from the Ministry to Thawin's house. As soon as he arrived he noticed that something was odd. Thawin was not sitting there waiting for him as she usually did. He looked around and, seeing no-one, took the liberty of stepping inside. There he saw Nai Rot sitting relaxing in his sarong, a sash draped over one shoulder. He was reclining with a bottle of whiskey and a glass beside him as always, puffing on a half-ashed cigarette. When he saw

Prince Lek he sat up abruptly, with a shock, drawing his sarong through his legs like a respectable loincloth and tying his sash neatly around his middle. He sat politely, legs to one side, hands in his lap. Prince Lek knew instantly that uncle Bunsom had told the family who he was. Nai Rot said haltingly, in ordinary, then royal, language, "You, I mean, Your Highness, has arrived."

Prince Lek sat down. Although Nai Rot had not asked him to, he took the liberty of doing what he was used to.

"Where's Thawin, uncle?" he asked.

"She's here . . . Your Highness." He spoke with difficulty, not knowing the correct forms. He called his daughter. Prince Lek already felt that the intimacy and informality which Nai Rot had shared with him had vanished, never to return. He was clearly regarded now as someone else, of different class and status, who had intruded into the heart of the jealously guarded family circle uninvited. They looked at each other in embarassed silence as they sat waiting for Thawin, no longer able to chat with their former ease. After a long time she came down and sat quietly, head bowed, at a distance. On his daughter's arrival, Nai Rot quickly got up and made his escape from the room, leaving them in the cold and lifeless atmosphere.

Thawin tried speaking to him in correct royal language, but the very effort of it, and the new language itself, made her seem alien, not the old Thawin he loved and wished to care for. As he listened to her speak, his hopes evaporated. She denied their past attachment, and when he reminded her of their previous understanding, answered that it was based on a mis-apprehension, as at that stage she had not known that he was of royal blood. She had not been trained in the ways of royalty and feared she would not be able to behave correctly.

"Even though I'm royal, I live like a commoner, because I'm not wealthy," he said to engage Thawin's sympathy, but she replied, "Then that's even worse. The neighbours will laugh at me if they know that I'm the consort of a prince but keep on living in the same old way, no better off."

FROM that time on Prince Lek felt that his life was dry, dessicated and meaningless. Happiness had been within reach, but the same old obstacle had snatched it away from him, with no chance of return. The distinction of his high birth, without the means of maintaining its differences, had turned into an evil ghost waiting to haunt him. It had already tormented his mother to death. This time it had returned, larger and more fearsome than before.

He stopped visiting Thawin's, and even found a different daily route to the Ministry to avoid passing her home. Each day he went to work, came home, and next day went to work again. His 'obstacle' dogged him like a shadow. Although he was only a government clerk, a relatively lowly position in the Ministry, his status was higher than his fellow clerks as well as his superiors. Communication was correspondingly awkward. He could not make any friends among the clerks. His superiors, when they found he was a prince, left him largely to his own devices, and did not supervise him or ask him to run errands. At a personal level, he had no way of becoming close and friendly with those above him. Sometimes when his boss had private functions at home—a party or the funeral of a benefactor or wife or children—the clerks would go along to help or try to curry favour with the boss, but Prince Lek had never gone along with them. This was not pride, but Prince Lek's sense of futility. Once he got there, he would have been seated in a place of honour and become the master himself.

The clerks who had come to help out would have to set cups of tea, hot water, betel nut and cigarettes in front of him, making him uneasy and even more awkward. The result of all this was that he was left alone in the crowd. In time, he became a forgotten person. No-one took any notice or interest in him, although they saw him every day. Everyone regarded him as they would a piece of furniture, such as a table or chair or an old file. When those who had started work along with him were promoted and leapt ahead in salary, he was still the old Prince Lek, in the same job, with a minimal rise in pay.

Prince Lek was buried among the old desks and papers, dried-up inkstands and rusty nibs, for over ten years. Most familiar faces had gone ahead in rank and status, leaving him behind in his old spot. Those ten years seemed like an age to him, more like half a century. Just as he had resigned himself to the prospect of moving neither up nor down for the rest of his life, uncle Bunsom fell ill and died.

Among the few possessions Uncle Bunsom left him was a plot of land of about twenty *rai*,* at Ban Tanot in the Chao Chet district of Suphan Buri province. Bunsom had purchased it as a young man, and left it in the care of an acquaintance. Prince Lek had not known that his uncle owned land, and only learned of it when it became his property after his uncle's death. That land became his dream. Another world, another existence, another realm. He could start again, unhindered by the dark shadow of his birth. Life would be cheerful in the midst of a community. A mixture of good and bad, they would certainly be better than nobody at all, better than being all alone in the world like a freak no-one wanted anything to do with. One day he disappeared from the Ministry and never

---

* About nine acres.

came back. After he had been absent for a month, still no-one knew or noticed, because once a person had been forgotten in his own lifetime, his presence or absence became equally immaterial.

ABOUT ten years later, if anyone asked about Headman Lek at Bang Tanot, they would be told immediately that he was headman of Village No. 11, which the locals called Ban O, in the Bang Tanot subdistrict. People who had been there for generations could add the information that headman Lek came from elsewhere. He had inherited the land at Ban O on the death of a relative, and had taken possession of it a few months later. Lek, the newcomer, was well-liked by the Ban O villagers and in the neighbourhood. He was good-natured, diligent, and hard-working. Apart from getting himself established, and expanding his area under cultivation, he was always ready to lend a hand to his neighbours. He never showed any objection to helping his fellows. He welcomed anyone in trouble or with a problem as he would a relative. There was no sorrow which he did not sympathize with; no problem too big for him to assist. Something about him made the villagers look up to and respect him. When the position of president of the temple fell vacant, the villagers presented it to Lek. Then when the old headman died, they elected Lek in his place, and everyone breathed a sigh of relief when he accepted. He lived alone, without a wife or children. There was talk that whenever he encountered an orphan he would adopt it to raise as his own, and that he now had a number of adopted children. When people asked about his family, Headman Lek would laugh and say, "I don't intend to have a family because I've got one already, and it's better than anyone else's! The whole of Ban O is my family."

Everyone who heard him speak like this was struck that he

said each word in a clear, resounding voice, as if distilled from a heart suffused with happiness and satisfaction.

BUT one day the assistant undersecretary came to the province on a tour of inspection, and came to the district. The district officer had instructed all elders and village headmen to line the way from the street in front of the district office to the water's edge to greet him. Lek was one of the village headmen who went along to form the receiving line.

It was a particularly hot and humid day, but even so everyone was neatly dressed in uniform. The elders and village headmen who had lined up to meet their superiors from the city all had great beads of sweat forming on their brows. Finally the sound of a ship's siren could be heard up the river, and after a flurry of movement from the Local Administration Department, the big steamship moored at the foot of the jetty in front of the district office. A large man dressed in inspection gear stepped imposingly out of the boat and shook hands with the district officer as though he were overwhelmingly pleased to see him.

As soon as he caught sight of the assistant undersecretary, Headman Lek started in fright. He felt so light-headed he nearly fainted in the sun. He remembered the man well. His name was Soem, and he had once sat at the desk next to Prince Lek's in the Ministry, as a clerk.

The assistant undersecretary made his way steadily along the receiving line, coming closer. Headman Lek stood with the sweat pouring down into his collar . . . The assistant undersecretary of the Ministry stopped and had a word with this headman and that elder in a loud and authoritative voice, like an adult speaking to a child. Sounds of hearty laughter erupted at intervals as he came closer, until eventually the group of civil servants led by the assistant undersecretary came to Headman Lek. The guest of honour looked as though he was going to walk straight past, but then Headman Lek started as if struck by lightning when he heard a voice say, so loudly that it was almost a shout, "Your Highness! How long have you been here? I haven't been in your royal presence for nearly twenty years! Do you remember me? My name is Soem, I used to work with Your Highness!"

That was all! Prince Lek reverted to the condition preceding his escape from city to country. Headman Lek died instantly with those few words, and Prince Lek returned to life to find hundreds of pairs of eyes staring at him as one. The hundreds of voices whispering to each other bore witness to him that his future existence in the Chao Ched region would be lonely. He would no longer be on the same informal terms. His continued existence in the region seemed without meaning or purpose.

Prince Lek sold his house and land and hurriedly caught the boat to Ban Phaen at night, to catch the passenger ferry to Bangkok. He sat jostled among strangers, the life before him obscured by the shadow of his royal birth, darker even than the storm beating down.

HIS body lay on the bank, unnoticed. There were no palace attendants, no flutes or drums or ceremonial instruments, to herald his death. That which had been an obstacle throughout his life was not there to accord him any honours in death. Someone remarked, "This old man must have come from another district. I've asked around and no-one seems to know him."

PHON—THE ACTOR

THERE was a time when everyone around Lat Pla Duk, past Phak Hai, had heard of Phon. For was it not his reputation as a leading folk actor that had once brought fame to the people of Lat Pla Duk?

Phon was born over fifty years ago, and had enjoyed acting in front of others for as long as he could remember. He performed better when there were interested spectators than when he did things on his own without an audience. Because of this, he had been sociable and gregarious from his earliest years. The crowds seemed an essential ingredient in allowing Phon to be himself, and without them his actions seemed to have no meaning.

Phon was one of the many children of a farming couple. Though not very rich, they were able to bring up all of their children on the understanding that once the children reached a useful age they would help with the farming or otherwise earn their keep. From the time Phon could run and swim, his parents set him the tasks of tending the buffaloes in the fields during the dry months, and of rowing out to collect grass for them in the wet season when they were under shelter. Phon loved to sing and dance and show off. He memorized the Choi songs, the boat songs, and folk opera ditties which the villagers liked to sing for pleasure, and sang them to the buffaloes out in the fields. But the buffaloes displayed little interest, continuing to bathe and chew their cud, and he had to find an audience elsewhere among the other young buffalo-tenders. At midday, after letting the buffaloes out into the fields, the few buffalo boys would gather to sit and chat under a clump of bamboo on a rise. It was at those times that Phon entertained his friends with his singing and dancing.

Phon's mother usually went to Phak Hai once or twice a month, to sell the fish that had been caught and kept in a basket in the water, because she got a better price than by selling them in front of her house; and to buy what she needed, for it was cheaper than buying from the boat vendor and there was a wider choice of goods. Once or twice she had taken Phon in the boat with her, and since then he had tried to cajole her into taking him every time she went. He had found a new and fascinating world at Phak Hai and longed for it with a burning desire. The wide, open fields of Lat Pla Duk which stretched as far as the eye could see, and the roofs which dotted the skyline, meant nothing to Phon. Even though it was his birth-place and since he had opened his eyes on the world he had known none but this landscape and atmosphere, he had never regarded Lat Pla Duk as his own, or himself as belonging to Lat Pla Duk. On the contrary, he felt constantly that other lives, other places in the world, forever beckoned him. Those worlds, those lives, were crowded with masses of people, filled with bright lights and the sounds of music and laughter. The emptiness of the fields, the sound of frogs croaking at night, of the breeze, of running water surrounding the house, held no power to bind his soul. But at Phak Hai, Phon had seen the gateway which led to the world he desired. There was a market with crowds of people coming and going, bright lights, sounds of song and laughter, and passenger boats plying up and down incessantly in confusion. The passenger boats carried goods and people, establishing contact between the provinces. Phon knew that these boats came from the vast world outside, the world he would step into one day, when he had the chance.

The event which determined Phon's life took place one day when he accompanied his mother to the Phak Hai market. There was a musical folk drama, *like*, at the market that day, put on by a famous company from Ayutthaya. People had been discussing it since midday, and the word was that to miss such an outstanding company was to have been born in vain. The company was going to perform at the market for three nights, so those who could spare the time had the opportunity to see their fill. Through her trading Phon's mother knew a fair number of people at the market. Everyone she bumped into was chattering about the *like*. They all urged her to stay on for it, but she replied noncommittally, "I didn't come alone, I've got young Phon with me. The opera won't be over till late, so it'd be a nuisance. I'd have to carry him down to the boat to go home, because he'll be asleep."

Someone said, "What does that matter? If he's asleep then he won't disturb us. On the way back you just have to put him in the boat, I don't see how it's any trouble."

Seeing his mother hesitate, Phon moved closer to her and said, "Stay for the *like*, Mother. Don't go home yet. I've never seen it, and I wouldn't mind."

But his mother went on buying and selling and did not reply. She stayed at the market the whole day. Phon did not go far, but scampered around close by her. He prayed anxiously that she would stay and watch the *like* and not go home. It was already late afternoon and he was concerned, fearing disappointment. His mother had long since sold all her vegetables and fish and bought all that she had to buy. Dusk was falling fast. Phon had eyes only for his mother's next move. Eventually she called him over and said, "You want to watch the folk opera, don't you Phon?"

His wish was too strong for him to express it in words. He could only nod his head. His mother understood and laughed, then said, "I'd like to see it too. Seeing we've come this far, the two of us, mother and son, we might as well stay on and watch. If your father gets mad at us for coming home late you'd better help make excuses for me!"

She picked up her purchases and put them in a basket which she left with a friend in the market. She told Phon that it was still early enough to find something to eat first. They each had a bowl of noodles. Phon could barely swallow his in his excitement. Then she paid the admission and took him through to sit in the thatched hall where the drama was playing. There were long benches for the audience. It was still light, and only a handful of people were scattered around. Not all the lamps had been lit yet, but as soon as he stepped into the hall the smell and atmosphere made him feel instantly that this was the world, the life, he had long wished and waited for. He sat beside his mother wide-eyed, staring fixedly at the performance stage. When the time came, a torn old backdrop was erected and two oil lamps were lit. The scene on the backdrop was a crudely drawn palace, but to Phon it was a goal, a symbol of the life he had always craved for even without knowing it.

Phon and his mother waited for some time. People gradually drifted in and greeted each other. Sounds of laughter and chatter surrounded him. Wherever he looked he saw the happy faces, freed from the tension of work and seeking diversion, eager to make the most of their happiness. Merely observing all the people around him excited Phon. He had never experienced such closeness to others. He had only seen people at home, or working, or going to and fro to buy and sell. He had seen them as ordinary and had not taken any interest or felt any intimacy and affection towards them. But the people who had gathered to watch the spectacle were a group whose mood he was seeing for the first time. He was just finding out how attractive his fellows were when so disposed, and how eminently desirable meeting them and establishing a rapport would be. Phon felt part of the group, with close and binding ties that would be difficult to sever.

The hall was nearly full. A murmur went up from the crowd. Phon craned his neck, but nothing was happening yet. A decrepit old man hung two additional lanterns, and turned up the others to make them brighter, making the raised platform which had been prepared for the folk opera into the single focus of illumination. He noticed some movement at the side of the hall, towards the front. Two or three people wandered out from the back and walked casually over to the array of traditional musical instruments. Some had the skinniness that was a sure sign of drug addiction; some were so old they could barely walk. Some were lighting up cigarettes, and others picked their teeth, showing that they had just eaten a good meal. Once the orchestra had taken its place, the noisy audience fell silent. Everyone looked eagerly ahead. A man sitting by a xylophone set up in front picked up the wooden stick and ran it gently over the keys, as if to give the pitch to those behind. The drummers, who were applying a paste of wet rice mixed with ash to their drums, softly tested the sound, enlivening the atmosphere in the theatre. The level of chatter fell even lower. The orchestra began to play the consecration, starting with a devotional song. At the first resonant sound of the drums, Phon's heart missed a beat, and from then on his every nerve seemed to move with the rhythm of the song, oblivious to everything else.

THINKING about it years later, Phon recalled that the *like* that night had not been as good as people had said. But at the time he did not yet know good from bad. He knew only that the vision the *like* left him with had quickened his heartbeat and aroused a greater variety of emotions than anything he had ever encountered. A life strange and beautiful to behold unfolded itself under the glow of a few lanterns. A life revolving around nobles and kings, dressed in glittering costumes. The single old backdrop behind the little stage was transformed from a magnificent palace to a forest setting, as the story cast its spell over him. The events that took place on those few boards fascinated him more than all the true stories in the world—tales or incidents that should have taken place over time were condensed; distances of hundreds and thousands of leagues from palace to forest, and from forest to goodness knows how many cities, were compressed into an easy walk three or four times round the stage and into the duration of the appropriate song. Every emotion, be it anger, resentment, sorrow, or gladness, had its own tune and lyrics, and even gestures, to embellish it and give it a clarity of outline beyond the emotions of real people he had known. Phon opened his heart to these things and let them seep through him as though someone had poured water on dry sand.

On the way home, as his mother worked the paddle at the rear of the boat, Phon sat at the prow with a feeling of happiness and satisfaction he had never before known. He sat bright-eyed, gazing into the darkness of the water. In that darkness he could still see the alternating hues, and the songs and music still echoed in his ears. The thing that gratified

him most was the close bond briefly shared with his fellows—
together they had laughed, felt saddened, and enjoyed themselves, seated next to one another, their hearts united by a
single focus—the story of the *like* taking place before them.

When they got home, his mother tied the boat to the head
of the steps and his father came to open the door. Phon walked
in and went to bed without saying a word. He heard his father
ask, "Where've you been all this time, Mother?"

"Phon wanted to watch the *like*, so I took him," his mother
said, shifting the blame onto Phon.

"You're always doing things like that," his father grumbled.
"He's only a kid. Take him to see these song and dance shows
and he'll end up with a passion for them and not want to work
for a living. Why go looking for trouble?"

His parents continued to debate the matter softly after Phon
had fallen asleep, lulled by the music of his own happiness. His
father could not know that Phon's passion was already beyond
the point of no return.

From then on, Phon was a changed person. Now he knew the
direction his life would take, and had cast away any indecision.
He would be a great king who would go off and study the
various arts at the feet of a sage. Then he would take leave
of his teacher and return home. On the way, he would meet
a damsel of overwhelming beauty in the midst of the forest.
He would enumerate her charms to sway the hundreds and
thousands of people in the audience; he would court her so
that the roars of appreciation could be heard for miles. Once
they had pledged their troth, a demon or bandit might try to
capture her, but no matter, Phon would fight without thought
for his life, until the curtain fell. Every man loved his wife, and
no-one who called himself a man would give her up without
a struggle! Later he might have to be separated from her, and

here his sorrow would move the audience to cry openly and cause even the flint-hearted to look away. Once he had gotten over his grief he would persevere with his search for his lady. Where he would meet her, and what would happen thereafter, would all be worked out the following day.

Tasks such as tending the buffaloes, catching fish, helping his parents in the fields, or scaring birds off the crops, became meaningless. He made himself do them to avoid a scolding, but all the while he was waiting for an opportunity—an opportunity he knew would come one day. During that time, Phon did many things which, had others seen them, they would have thought bizarre. Alone in the house, he furtively powdered his face and contemplated the effect in the mirror. He made his face up, using an incense stick dipped in water to colour his mouth and baked ash from the bottom of the cooking pot to accentuate his eyebrows and paint beauty spots. Watching himself in the mirror he would try smiling or looking angry, then hurriedly wash the makeup off for fear someone might see him. Even so, he thought that with powder and makeup, he was better looking than most. He was most contented when fishing, or cutting grass in the fields by himself, as then he could practise the actions he had seen and still remembered and sing the recollected snatches of song at the top of his voice without being disturbed or rebuked.

TIME moved inexorably on, from months to years. One year became two, then three and four. Phon stayed in the same place. Yet he did not mind, sustained by his unflinching faith in his own destiny. His parents tried to train him to cultivate the land so that he could support them in their dotage, not knowing that he had other plans. People can plan ahead for many things, but we cannot prevent, obstruct or alter our fate or fortune. When Phon was just over sixteen, the opportunity he had awaited so patiently came to him.

*Thit** Plian, a well-off villager, was about to mark his son's ritual entry into the monkhood with a lavish celebration. He sent for a good *like* troupe from Suphan province. The director and the hero were one and the same person, Nai Thapthim, whose fame had extended not only to Phak Hai, but over the fields to Lat Chado, Lat Pla Duk and Lat Namkham. The *like* was going to play for three days. Thit Plian wanted to celebrate to the full his joy at having raised his only son to the age of ordination. Phon knew Thit Plian's household well, and was friendly with the young postulant. When preparations for the celebrations commenced, Phon spent all his time helping out. His parents did not complain—it was generally accepted that when people had work or festivities to organize, their friends would lend a hand, if not with money then with labour.

Phon volunteered to wait on the performers, so he had the chance to see the backstage lives of the folk opera troupe at close quarters. He took their trays of food back stage, and brought them water or whisky when required. During the performances he sat at the back of the stage, and watched their every pose. He was pleased to see that their existence was entirely separate from that of the ordinary villager, a new world, created anywhere they put up their stage. Life in this new world was replete with happiness and sorrow, love and friendship, jealousy, rivalry and quarrels. Their lives did not start with sunrise, cock's crow and bird song—daytime was for sleep, and the new day started with lamplight and orchestral fanfare. Everyone embarked on this life with powder, face paint,

---

* Shortened form of *bandit*, 'the learned one', used when addressing a man who has been ordained.

and brightly coloured costumes, and then waited the allotted time backstage for the rhythm of life to begin. There were no troubles, no problems to worry over. Phon was honoured to be close to that life, and by the third day he knew that it would be an inseparable part of his own.

Straight after the third night's performance, the troupe hurriedly packed up their belongings, as the manager, Nai Thapthim, said he had promised to perform in Ayutthaya the following night. When they had packed, they left in the boats that were waiting and rowed hurriedly to reach their destination at the appointed time. They passed Lat Chado in darkness, Phak Hai near dawn, and it was not until the full light of day shone over the water that some of those who had been sleeping rolled over and opened their eyes and saw Phon sitting at the back of the boat. They raised the alarm.

"What's your name, and where are you from?" Thapthim was the first to ask, after he had been told that there was a strange young man in the boat.

"My name is Phon, and I'm from Lat Pla Duk," he answered, and went on to say, "I served all your meals and waited on you backstage at the house where they had the celebrations. Don't you remember me, Phi?"

"That's right," Thapthim recalled, "and where are you off to?"

"I want to go with you and learn to act in the *like*. Do take me on—you can set me to any task, I won't mind."

"It's not easy, being an actor, and you have to look the part," Thapthim said. "I don't know yet whether you'll be able to. Do you have parents? And if you do, do they know that you've come with me?"

"My parents are both alive," Phon replied frankly. "I didn't tell anyone when I left. When I saw you boarding the boat, I just jumped in. I barely knew what I was doing. I must just be drawn to this kind of life."

"Mmh," Thapthim exclaimed softly, "You're like me when I was a kid. I ran after them like that because I loved it, only I didn't have any father and mother. What will you say if your parents come looking for you?"

"Even if they did, I probably wouldn't go back. Anyway, they've got so many children they might not come after me."

Thapthim laughed, and said, "This guy's a pretty smart talker." He inclined his head to one side and scrutinized Phon's face and figure critically, as if he were picking him up and examining him, then mentally weighing him like someone buying fish or vegetables. Finally he said, "Your face and figure aren't bad—it's hard to say, you might be able to make a go of it—anyway it's already too late to take you back. As you want to join us, you can, but if your parents come for you, it's none of my business. You sort it out yourselves."

Phon was so relieved and delighted that if Thapthim had not turned over to go back to sleep when he had finished speaking he would have prostrated himself before him.

From then on, Phon followed Thapthim's *like* troupe everywhere, from north to south, in theatres, at temple fairs, in open fields. Sometimes he encountered extravagance on a scale he had never seen before, when everyone seemed wealthy enough to buy wide gold rings and thick gold chains to wear. At other times he experienced unimagined poverty, with barely enough rice to feed the troupe, and any chains or rings, or even clothes, speedily whisked away to the pawn shop. Occasionally they had to escape from the theatre in the dead of night because they could not find the rent money.

Phon began his new life by being useful back stage. He helped to cook and carry, and beat the drum to call everyone to the joint meal at the appropriate time. He ran to buy sweets and cigarettes and alcohol as his elders called for them. When the opera was playing, he sat backstage and watched the others act. He never tired of this, and memorized all the lyrics and movements. He took special note when director Thapthim was on stage, hardly taking his eyes off him, softly mouthing the songs and mimicking his every attitude and gesture. Every time the crowd applauded his heart beat faster, as if that sound were an admiring response to his own acting. In a short time he had thrown himself into his new life body and soul, as if he had been born to the stage. As he went to sleep, he paid homage to the early teachers venerated by all performers. He bowed every time he passed the image of the sage, symbol of the first teacher, and made obeisances each time he touched it. Every evening he lit a candle and incense and paid his respects. Musical sounds did not merely please him as before, but became important and essential elements of life. The sounds of the drums were the rhythm and beat of life, the beating of the heart which, while it lasted, signified that all was well with the body. Each song had its own meaning which touched the heart and aroused the emotions. Some were exalted and sacred, like the consecration, the Khom Wian, and the Tra Nimit. When he heard these his whole being experienced a shiver of awe, and he automatically raised his hands in prayerful salutation. Phon did not regard the profession of a folk actor, or song and dance act as his father once called it, as something lowly or even simply enjoyable, but as important, esteemed, and sacrosanct, worthy of exaltation and preservation even with one's life. The stage encompassed everything in the world outside, and its own particular versions of these as well—from religion, ethics and administration, to traditions and notions of ambition, love, anger and revenge. It seemed as though these things from the external world had been compressed and intensified, giving them a completely different flavour, difficult for outsiders to understand.

Phon was especially interested in three people in the company. The first was the stage manager, Thapthim. As Phon had placed himself in Thapthim's hands it was natural that he should be conscious of his importance. Second was Plot, the principal xylophone—*ranat*—player. Phon was interested in him only because he had a daughter, Phen, who accom-panied him everywhere. An innocent sweet girl, two or three years younger than Phon, she was the third person who interested him.

Thapthim smoked opium,* as he maintained that it develop-ed keenness of mind and beautified the figure and complexion as befitted a theatrical manager. Plot, on the other hand, drank, as he asserted that without alcohol he could not lift the xylophone sticks, or even if he could, the resulting tune would be dry and flat rather than smooth and brisk as it should be. Phon took care of the needs of both Thapthim and Plot in these matters. He lit the lamp and set the pipe up in the afternoon, and rolled the opium and held it over the flame until done. Then he put it in the hollow reed pipe which Thapthim lay holding in readiness, and stayed there until the director began to feel satisfied. Thapthim was in the habit of dozing, giving him tips on acting, getting him to memorize various verses and charms, or telling him anecdotes of life on the stage. Every time he served Thapthim, Phon learnt things of interest to him. For Plot, Phon ran and bought liquor before the afternoon meal. Sometimes he sat and listened to Plot chat about the one subject he spoke of when drunk, his

* Smoking opium was legal in Thailand until 1957.

own life as chief *ranat* player in themusical circles of various nobles in Bangkok, and when he had taken up with Phen's mother, and how he was betrayed by her when she ran off with another man, leaving their only daughter for him to raise. His sense of injury had prevented him from having another wife or child. Instead he had hauled Phen from pillar to post, playing his music, until he ended up in Thapthim's troupe, which he referred to contemptuously as the 'bumpkin opera'.

Other members of the troupe changed constantly. Old faces disappeared, were replaced by new ones, then changed again. Phon saw this as routine and did not take much notice, but one day after one of the young men who played a supporting role had vanished Thapthim said, "Phon, do you think you could try going on stage tonight?"

Phon nearly fell where he stood with excitement and pleasure, and answered hesitantly in a trembling voice, "Well—it's up to you—if you say I can then I can."

Plot, who was lounging around listening, interrupted and said, "Hey, don't pretend false modesty, young Phon. I've been watching you for a while. I can tell, you've got more style than a lot of others."

Phon turned to Plot and smiled with pleasure. Thapthim said, "Okay. Tonight you can be one of the officials. It's not hard, there's no singing. Just do what the others do for now. If you do well, later on I'll let you play other roles and teach you the parts."

That day Phon felt as though he were floating, and whatever he looked at seemed fresh and delightful. His status had changed to performer. He felt at once that he held more privileges than before in the world behind the scenes. Even though his first role was a minor one, he was not disheartened. He knew he had plenty of time ahead.

That night he made up himself painstakingly and dressed with the skill and speed of an experienced performer. When the orchestra started with the consecration, Phon lit a candle and incense to pay respect to the ancient masters with single-minded concentration. Plot washed the surface of the drum with a glass of whisky and then passed him a small glassful. Thapthim called him over to kneel before him with hands folded in prayer, then mumbled an incantation and blew three times onto the centre of his head. Each time Phon felt a cold shiver down his spine. His hair stood on end from the awesome power of the master, and every muscle trembled. Thapthim then blessed a chew of betel nut for him, marking the end of the ritual. He was ready to perform.

Phon had a minor part that night and did not have much acting to do. He was only an official, attending on and following the hero in time to the beat of the songs. He waited and watched, and cheered when Thapthim did battle with the villain. Every time Phon looked at the audience, his heart swelled. Hundreds and thousands of eyes were fixed with interest on the stage; he could see a sea of heads in the theatre. They followed every action of those under the stage lights. Phon knew that he was performing not just on stage, but in the hearts and emotions of the audience single-mindedly gathered there. He knew that one day he would be able to use the power of this position to force masses of people to laugh or cry, as he pleased. His time would come one day.

From then on Phon appeared on stage every day. At first Thapthim taught him the parts to commit to memory. When, shortly after, the time came to progress from an official to other minor characters, Thapthim arranged for him to play as his brother or friend. Phon acted to the best of his ability, with feeling, taking care not to look awkward or to go beyond the confines of the role. The parts Thapthim taught him were basic ones he already knew well, like that for courting a lady.

"See the front—gold plated; see the back—just like silver. I'm in love with you, my painted beauty. I'm keen, oh lady dressed in yellow."

Phon sang these parts fluently and fast without stumbling, pleasing Thapthim and making Plot laugh with amusement, showing his gums and playing the *ranat* with greater finesse than usual. Phon studied the songs unobtrusively, to the point where he could use words with the accents of the special *likae* dialogue. For instance, 'gold' had to be 'gol-l-l', with the emphasis on a final 'l', and 'silver' had to be 'silverl-l-l'. So as time went on Thapthim came to trust him, and only had to tell him which character he was playing for him to come up with the appropriate actions and songs. He no longer needed supervision.

In the next four or five years Phon became more and more independent. During the early stages, his acting followed conventional stereotypes, or his recollections of performances by others, but after a while he began to make a name for himself with his own method. People knew him as Phon, not just as an actor in Thapthim's troupe, and wherever they performed there would be some who came especially to see him.

It is a law of nature that there is only one leader in any group. But the leader can only remain if not displaced by one younger, stronger and more able, who will fight until the old leader is defeated. When people form groups or communities and live together according to simple rules, they often unconsciously fall back on these laws of nature.

To tell the truth, Phon recognized the debt he owed Thapthim for nurturing him and teaching him all he knew, but his desire to be independent and to display his own talents made him start unintentionally competing with Thapthim on stage. When they appeared in the same scene, if Thapthim sang a basic melody, Phon would respond artlessly with a song in a higher key, or he would cut in and prevent Thapthim from finishing. Knowing that *like* most gripped its audience in the final scenes when the orchestra took up the refrain he would snatch that part for himself. Even more importantly, while Thapthim was singing or dancing, he would seize the limelight and become the focus of attention, relegating his master to a supporting role. Two people egged Phon on—Plot and Phen.

Phon had observed Phen since she was a young girl. By the time she had grown up, he was in the full flush of manhood and his actions showed that he loved her. Phen was not averse to establishing the ties of love and desire with him. He was young, better looking than most, and seemed assured of a future as a prosperous manager of a theatrical troupe. Plot preferred Phon to Thapthim because as his daughter's lover, Phon deferred to him. Unlike Thapthim, who saw himself as the star and the manager and behaved arrogantly towards Plot, Phon listened to his every word.

Initially Phon performed to win acclaim so that he could show off to Phen, his loved one, and Plot only backed him up robustly through the sound of his *ranat*.No matter what Phon sang or danced, Plot played to the hilt every time, with great style, unlike the indifferent way he played for others. With Phon's youth, his looks, the wit and deportment he strove to perfect, and the enhanced beauty of Plot's music, he became one of the most prominent actors in the troupe, although Thapthim was still the principal. At a later stage, Plot and Phen changed from support to incitement. When Plot had had a few drinks he would say, "Phon! You're still young and fit, and your skills are second to none! How long are you going to put up with playing second fiddle?"

Phen would echo her father and say, "That's right. I can tell that if you were the lead people would really fall for you. Look at me, I'm infatuated, and I've been with the *like* since I was a child. It's a pity Thapthim won't let you be the star just because he wants to be. In fact I don't think he's as good as you. He's way behind."

The two of them egged Phon on, and gradually he succumbed to their pressure. He forgot his debt of gratitude to Thapthim and began to consider ways of getting rid of him. Seeing Phon's acquiescence, Plot changed his tactics from encouragement to helping him bring Thapthim down. Phon began to cut him out on stage without a qualm. When Thap-thim played a tragic or romantic hero, Phon made the audience laugh, or stood to one side facing them and put on a dumb-show to make him look like a clown. When Thapthim sang the plot, Phon interrupted and changed the lyrics, so that he looked foolish. For instance, when Thapthim was the hero, and Phon his younger brother, Thapthim would sing the part where he was in the forest looking for his love in the following way: "Beloved brother, we've travelled long through the forest, and been gone from home all these days, but not yet encountered a fair maiden. I think continually of my royal parents. They'll be beset with anxiety as they search for us. We must go back to the capital to seek an audience."

Thapthim looked as though he was going to sing on. He was on the point of leading the orchestra into the refrain when Phon cut in with, "It's all very well to talk, but who's going to pay the fare, brother. I'm broke and in debt for a cup of tea myself !"

Plot responded on the *ranat* with pride and satisfaction.

Amidst the resounding laughter of the audience Thapthim lost considerable ground and Phon boosted his standing.

As well as this, Plot helped Phon demolish Thapthim in front of everybody through his *ranat* playing.Sometimes Plot would accompany Thapthim's singing with a melody so off key that it made him sound as though his voice was failing and he was unable to harmonize with the orchestra. At other times Plot pretended carelessness in not accompanying a song until it was over. Thapthim was left looking awkward on stage or stammering on with his extemporising, with all the earlier harmonies lost. Sometimes before the end when he stopped only long enough to swallow, Plot played on regardless so that he could not sing the song as he had planned, through to its conclusion.

Bickering and quarrels between Thapthim, on one side, and Phon and Plot on the other, continued with increasing frequency. One day after leaving the stage, Thapthim, bitterly resentful, coughed up blood. He left at dawn, after accusations of ingratitude and a night of stinging exchanges. Only two of the troupe went with him. The entire orchestra and most of the actors elected to stay with Phon, and elevated him to be the lead and manager in Thapthim's stead.

That day was one of Phon's happiest. He had fulfilled his lifelong aspirations. "Nai Phon's *Like* Troupe", or "There it is! Phon's *like*" were music to his ears, and never ceased to move him. Those words resounded inwardly all that day, whatever he was doing. Phon and his team agreed to break for a few days to find new props and costumes, as Thapthim had walked off with all the old ones. They had had a good run recently, and everyone had money in their pockets which would last them for some time. That night, after a victory celebration sodden with drink, Plot said drunkenly as Phon was getting up to go off to bed, "Hey Phen, what are you sitting around for? Go and see to Phon's bed for him, and don't come back, either. Stay close at hand to take care of him, so he can call on you if he needs anything in the night."

When Phon blew out the lamp and entered his mosquito net, Phen willingly laid her warm body down next to his.

DURING the ten years that followed, Phon's stars were in the ascendant. No-one called him 'young Phon' or 'that Phon' or even plain 'Phon'. Everyone referred to him as 'Elder Brother Phon' or 'Mr. Phon', and to the older *like* devotees he was '*Pho** Phon'. Not long after he parted company with Thapthim, Phon became renowned for his ability to draw huge audiences everywhere he went. At that time, 'Mr. Phon's *like*' and 'actor Phon' were household words throughout the provinces. His fame spread from southern Prachuap up to Phetchaburi, Ratchaburi, Nakhon Chaisi, Suphan, Ang Thong, and Ayutthaya. People gathered wherever he performed. Especially around Phak Hai, Lat Chado, and Lat Pla Duk, almost the whole subdistrict would turn out. They knew Phon was a local boy who had gone away and made a name for himself, and took pride in his achievement. He did not repudiate this, and every time he played at or near home he performed to the fullest extent of his abilities.

People who had seen him perform related anecdotes of the impact of Phon at his peak. Some old ladies in the audience were wont to fan themselves with one hand while raising betel nut chews to their mouths with the other, never stopping. The moment Phon appeared, the fans stopped at the same time as

---

* Literally, 'father'. In this context it is used as a term of endearment that older *like* admirers use to address a younger actor.

the hands feeding the betel chews froze rigid in mid-mouthful, not to move again until he left the stage. One old lady used to attend every night of his performance. She would come early and lie down to sleep comfortably on her side on a long bench, with instructions to the children who accompanied her to wake her only when Phon was on stage.

The elderly were not Phon's only admirers. He was popular with men, women and children of all ages because he performed in his own lively and inimitable fashion. He lived only to perform, to appear before his one great love, his audience. His love and affection for the audience seemed to call forth a similar response. Phon never failed to play to his audience, making them feel closely involved with events on stage rather than simply spectators. He was enquiring and observant. He always managed to work any special features pertaining to the village or subdistrict where he was performing into his plot. For instance, the people of Ban Lat Chado and Lat Pla Duk shared the perception that inhabitants of the former were grander and more prosperous, but no-one had captured it in choice words that became common parlance. So when Phon performed at his old home and sang, "Lat Chado is full of the rich, their houses roofed with corrugated iron. My home is poor, covered in thatch and stubble," he dug deep into the emotions of the people of Lat Pla Duk and gave them expression in song. And when he finished the song, the applause echoed through the fields in the way he had always hoped to hear. His secret was not in chants or incantations, but in the few simple words that endeared him to people and moved them so profoundly. When a description was required, Phon refused to go on at length, drawing instead on objects familiar to the local people to illustrate his meaning with sharp-edged clarity.

Once Phon played a hero forced by circumstance to leave at

dawn after he had slept only a single night with the heroine. Phon did not moan and sob at length as others would have in the parting song, because he knew that would bore the audience and leave them unmoved. When it came to the part in the play where his night with the heroine was coming to an end, towards dawn, he sang only a few words but they touched the audience deeply. The verse was simply this: "Rooster, don't crow; sun, don't rise; so that I can hold this soft body, to the full, for just one night."

Anyone who took the trouble to examine these words would see how much Phon, the hero, loved the heroine. For the sake of that love, he begged for the impossible, even to imploring the cock not to crow, so as to prolong their only night together.

Sometimes Phon used sarcasm to satirize individuals or events he knew the audience disliked. When he performed at Pak Tho he noticed a large shop in front of the theatre. The shopkeeper's name was Khun Nai Kim Rian. At night, before the opera closed down, the shop would be brightly lit, and old Khun Nai Kim Rian would powder her face and sit in the glare as she had done as a girl, decades ago. She was an arrogant woman, who held herself aloof because of her wealth and did not get on with most of the villagers. They were disgusted by her, especially for making up her face at her age. After a few days Phon sensed the feeling of the local audience, and one night he came on stage and said, "Phon's here at last—why don't you buy a ticket, my darling Kim Rian? If you wait too long your face will darken!"

The response to this short verse was deafening. The direct appeal of the words was such that once heard they were memorized, and the sound of asking and retelling rippled through the hall. Within moments Phon's verse had left the theatre, and rounds of applause could be heard as far away as the back of the market. The only person not amused was *Khun Nai* Kim Rien.

PHON prospered in name and fame for over ten years, with Nang Phen, his wife, by his side. Plot, her father, had died. Phon had no vices. He was not addicted to opium or alcohol. He was not a gambler nor a philanderer. His utmost satisfaction was gained from performing opera, and he wanted nothing more. He handed all his earning over to Nang Phen, who was by now middle-aged.

Yet either nature's law of the survival of the fittest, or the retribution of fate, determined that as Phon grew older his looks were not as fresh, nor his voice as clear and resonant, as before. The things he had once done to Thapthim were now being done to him.

A young boy from Bangkok named Thomya, slender and with flawless looks, had attached himself to Phon's troupe as a performer. Phon took him on because he had acting experience. After Thomya had been there only a month, Phon realized his mistake, but was unable to remedy the situation. Thomya had contrived to curry favour with Phen, who had become hopelessly infatuated with him, and Phon was under his wife's sway.

From then on the old sequence of rivalry and betrayal began all over again. Phon attempted to fight back, knowing all the while that he was not up to it. Despite the fact that his intelligence and wit were still sharp, he could not compete with Thomya in youth and good looks. In addition, Thomya was known to be a Bangkok performer and had a distinctive style, which gave him an edge over Phon every time. Phon had to bide his time patiently for many months. Everything that happened showed a blatant intent, and when one day he found that Thomya had overstepped the mark even with his own wife, he called a meeting of the whole troupe. He announced that he would withdraw and transfer all rights to Phen. At the same time he suggested that the new lead should be none other than Thomya.

Phon crawled back to his home in Lat Pla Duk like a wounded animal. His father had died a long time ago, leaving only his mother and younger brothers and sisters, who were all grown up. His family seemed to understand without needing to inquire. Phon lay in hiding quietly at home for many years, as if resting up to heal wounds deep in his heart. During that time his theatrical reputation faded. No-one spoke of him, and his place was taken by other troupes and other stars.

Phon, whom the children now called 'Grandfather Phon' or 'Uncle Phon' used to lie and listen to his brother Phan's radio. One night as he lay listening without paying much attention one item made him sit up and take notice, his hair standing on end. Someone on the radio was saying distinctly that the government would promote the performance of musical drama or *like*. There was to be an *like* competition on the radio. Whichever troupe performed best would receive a gold trophy from the prime minister. Hot blood started to race through his body. Right! Nobody could see how old you were on the radio, they only listened to the voice and words. Phon was certain of one thing—that no-one could beat him. Radio *like*! Radio *like*! What a clever idea! Come what may, he would have to enter that competition. This time his voice would resound over all Thailand, letting people know that Phon the actor was still around, his fame still undiminished . . .

Phon took the little boat to Ban Phaen the next morning. His fellow passengers did not know where he was going, nor had he even told his relatives back home. He wanted everyone to find out for the first time through the voice over the radio

which would ring out to the farthest riverbanks th
actor had returned once more.

When the passenger ferry that ran between Ban Phaen a
Bangkok capsized, Phon was going over opera parts in his
head. He was cheerful and unworried, and as carefree as he had
been once upon a time in his youth when he ran away from
home to join the troupe. But his body was too old to swim
against the waves.

An old villager saw his body on the riverbank in the morning
and said wistfully, "Look, this is Phon, the actor. All he did was
to make people laugh and have fun. He's never done any harm.
Why did he have to die like this?"

–THE DAUGHTER

FROM as far back as she could remember, Lamom had no recollection of what her father was like. She knew only that her mother's name was Lamun and that she had lived all her life in a two-storey wooden shophouse in the market of Sena district. Her mother, Nang Lamun, sold odds and ends in the shop below, and they lived upstairs. Apart from her earnings from the sale of dry goods downstairs, Nang Lamun had some income from the rental of land. Although not much, it was enough for the two of them, mother and daughter.

Lamom had always known that she was different from everyone else. It was her mother, Nang Lamun, who set her apart. Lamom had no memories of maternal love; the only thing she knew, and that she felt all the time, was the burden of Nang Lamun's parental care constantly weighing her down both in body and spirit.

When Lamom was young her mother used to tell her that her father had been a government official, with the rank of *luang*.[*] He had been a district officer, a respected and prominent figure

---

[*] A non-hereditary title bestowed on a government official of a middle-level rank used before the constitutional monarchy began in 1932.

in the community. He died shortly after Lamom's birth. His wife and daughter were left in difficulty. Nang Lamun had to return to her old home in Sena district, and maintained a livelihood from the rental of the land her husband had bought her and by trading in small dry goods.

"Even though we're poor, we're not dependent on anyone for a living," Nang Lamun would say to her daughter. "If Khun Luang, your father, was still alive we wouldn't be like this. You should know you're the daughter of a gentleman, of a good family, not like these wild kids who run around the market. You have to keep yourself to yourself and on no account mix with them, because you're a gentleman's daughter. I've had a hard time earning a living since your father died, because of you. If I didn't have you I'd have been comfortable ages ago, but because of you I have to put up with all sorts of hardship. I live for you—you should be mindful of my sacrifices, and you'd better not forget it!"

Lamom's mother had never shown her any affection, although she told her constantly that she loved her and commented incessantly on the debt her daughter owed her. She maintained that it was her daughter's duty to be mindful of her goodness and to repay this massive debt. Lamom had never known love that was all-giving and demanded nothing in return, had never known the maternal love that would do anything for a child without a thought of the sacrifice involved. Even so, when she was younger she hardly knew, or loved, anybody else, and if anyone had asked her who she loved, she would have said her mother. Had she been able to explain, she might have said she never wanted to love anyone else in her whole life, because love as she experienced it was a heavy burden, requiring never-ending recompense through every waking moment. It could be said that the only time left to Lamom for herself was when she was asleep.

Nang Lamun was fatter than most, so the burden of her love bore down both emotionally and in a material sense. Since she became aware, Lamom could remember hardly anything in her life other than having to wait on this huge lump of flesh covered in fat, this living lump of flesh which called itself mother. Lamom used to peek out at other children playing cheerfully, then turn away. Not only was she forbidden to play with the 'wild kids', she knew she would not be able to find the time to. She had to sweep the house, do the washing, cook the rice, and run out for snacks or betel nut for her mother at intervals throughout the day. What little time she had left was spent sitting fanning her mother, or treading on her, or massaging her. There was no end to these activities. Sometimes Lamom stubbornly sat and played elsewhere, or went for a walk, but the sound of a voice shouting "Lamom" dogged her footsteps until her will to get away was broken, and she set her face to return home, hopelessly.

Nang Lamun never beat her daughter when she thought she had done wrong, but to Lamom her method of punishment was far worse than being beaten or scolded. Nang Lamun's punishment was to go cold and refuse to speak to her or ask her to do things. Lamom had to sit at home doing nothing, her eyes following her mother as she heard her slow form move around attending to things. Her mother would wheeze loudly or moan all the while, so that Lamom would hear how much she had to suffer and tire herself. She would perform these tasks without speaking to Lamom for about half an hour, or an hour at the most. As she went along her wheezing would get heavier, or her moaning louder, and she would be bathed in sweat with her hair awry. When she felt she had reached a pitch of fatigue she would cry out, "Help, I'm fainting!" or some other exclamation, loudly enough for Lamom to hear, and then lie down then and there on the spot. Lamom would have to come to the rescue with cold water and smelling salts until Nang Lamun opened her eyes, then she would have to half carry, half support her walking to bed.

Then she would sit by her side fanning her as her mother lay with tears streaming down her face, bemoaning how cruelly fate had treated her. The death of her husband when she was still young, the ingratitude of her child, created overwhelming difficulties for her at this age. Had she not had children and not had to give her life over to her only child, who knows how her life would have been. Nang Lamun would evoke such a perfect vision that even Lamom, who had heard it all before, never failed to be carried away. She always ended her monologue with a plea to her daughter to repay her debt to her beloved mother with all her heart and soul, and even with her whole life. When Lamom showed signs of guilt and repentance, and agreed not to repeat her offence, Nang Lamun would signal her forgiveness by sitting up and giving Lamom money to buy either fish custard, curry, or a half bottle of liquor. Nang Lamun would eat heartily, claiming that her faintness had whetted her appetite. As for alcohol, it was a necessary medicine. With her weak heart she never knew when she might faint again, so had to guard against the possibility with a few drinks.

As Lamom grew older, the main burden of her life, her mother, seemed to grow with her. When she was little she only had to do those tasks which her mother told her to, but as she grew to adolescence, she had to shoulder the entire burden of work within the household—the marketing, the cooking, the fetching of water, the washing and the cleaning, as well as waiting on the whims of Nang Lamun. With the passing of the years Nang Lamun had let her body run to fat and flesh to an incredible extent, and now hardly moved at all. She lay in her room upstairs with a bottle of 'medicinal' liquor at her side, and called incessantly on Lamom to wait on her. She only came downstairs to take a bath, or to see whether anyone was visiting Lamom.

Although Lamom was now a young woman, she seemed older than her years. Her body, instead of beaming with health as she grew, like others of her age, became gaunt and parched. Her skin, her eyes, and her hair seemed devoid of life. In fact she could have been as pretty as other young girls, but the nature of her existence and the heavy burden in her life made her unattractive. She made no effort to beautify herself, because she had given way to despair, and saw no meaning in life apart from enslavement to her own mother. Age and the passage of time did not lessen Nang Lamun's demands on Lamom in the slightest. On the contrary, they increased with every passing hour and minute. Nang Lamun's body, which grew fatter by the day, called out for food of great quantity and quality. Every time Lamom put food down in front of her she would complain as she ate it.

"Lamom! This soup is insipid and flavourless. No matter how often I tell you, it doesn't sink in!" she would say to her daughter. "The chili sauce is so sour it sets my teeth on edge! How many times do I have to tell you to go easy on the lemon juice? What's this? Bean salad? Heavens! It's like something you're about to throw out! You know I like you to put a lot of coconut cream in it. How stingy can you be! What kind of a child are you, mean to your own mother?" Then she would stop and have a gargle of liquor and go on to bewail her fate—that in this life she could not have the kind of child she wanted, although she had sacrificed her whole life for her daughter.

"If I hadn't had you when Khun Luang died," she would

start to say, "I'd be happy by now. I was young then, not old like now, and I had a bit of money. Plenty of good young men were interested in me. If I'd remarried, I wouldn't have had to live in poverty like this, but I didn't because I loved you. I felt sorry for you, and thought that a stepfather might maltreat you. I endured patiently great hardship, and wept floods of tears while I brought you up. Seeing there are only two of us I thought I'd live with you till I died. I never thought my daughter would be so cruel as to think of leaving me, and that she could barely be bothered to do anything for me. Even the cooking tastes like it's done for a pig or a dog."

Having said this much she would stop and sob, tears streaming down her face, then go on, "This is what they call 'a tree dying from its fruits'. I never thought it would happen to me. I don't know what I did in my past lives to deserve this!"

When Lamom heard a tirade like this she put her head down and collected her mother's cups and plates and took them downstairs to wash. As she went down the stairs her mother's voice would follow her, shouting, "Evil daughter! I can't say a word without you looking sulky. Banging the cups and plates around as if you were a millionaire minting money and breakages didn't matter!"

Then Lamom, working downstairs, would hear sobs and moans from upstairs, along with the clink of liquor bottle against glass, the sound of liquor being poured into the glass, and finally the cry, "Help! I'm fainting!" This was the signal for her to drop everything and run upstairs to cajole and care for her mother once again.

LAMOM lived like this for many years, and had it not been for the war and the ensuing inflation, she might have continued to do so. But when it came to making her living, or rather her mother's living, the war and its aftermath had left Lamom hard up. Nang Lamun still demanded the same amount of food and accoutrements to good living as before, yet the amount of money she gave Lamom was still the same. Lamom did everything she could to make ends meet, but as time went on the money seemed increasingly worthless. As food and personal belongings grew scarce, Nang Lamun cursed and scolded her daughter even more frequently. In the past, Lamom had never argued with her mother. But when she was accused of embezzling money for personal use or of being spendthrift, after a while she had to make excuses, and when her mother did not believe her but continued to abuse her, excuses turned to arguments. These arguments were fuelled by anger and hurt, emotions she had never before experienced.

Previously she had considered waiting on her mother to be a necessary part of life, something she had to put up with despite the hardship and tiredness. Later, the poverty and shortages gradually made her see life with her mother as an almost unbearable burden. The fate which she had seen as giving her an opportunity to make merit by serving her progenitrix slowly began to seem evil. Instead of creating understanding or cementing the bond between mother and daughter, everything she did for the sake of her mother and everything she had put up with aroused her suspicions and increased the distance between them by leaps and bounds. Like most people, Lamom wanted her virtue to be appreciated and reciprocated. She interpreted the saying 'good rewards for good deeds, evil returns for evil deeds' literally, without close analysis, so that when she was good to her mother, she hoped for good from her in return. When after many years the good that she wished for had not taken shape or form, her feelings began to change. She felt slighted in her lot, her emotions shaken and easily affected.

One day, after Lamom had attempted to explain to her mother that the quality and quantity of food had declined because goods were more expensive and that the money her mother gave her now and then was insufficient for their needs, and after Nang Lamun had spent a suitably long time crying and bemoaning her fate, she mentioned through her sobs that, "We get poorer every day . . . soon we'll die of starvation, or have to go out to beg . . . I might as well not have a child. Other children see their mothers living in poverty and go out to earn a living to help, but my child only helps spend. Whatever is given is never enough, because she thinks she's well born and can't work. She wouldn't even think of helping enough for both of us . . . " and went on sobbing.

Lamom suppressed her anger for a moment, then said, "What more do you want me to do? My hands are full with housework every day, I barely have any spare time as it is."

"Oh, don't carry on, your ladyship," her mother said sarcastically. "I'm in poor health and you look after me a bit and nearly die with the effort and can't do anything else. Great Lamom! Seeing as you get so tired of looking after me, I'll hurry up and die! I won't prolong your troubles much longer. I didn't know my child would turn out to be an ogre, a demon, starving her mother! I'll die soon so you can live well, don't worry." She cried and sobbed so loudly as she spoke that the layers of fat on her body rippled.

"Really, Mother, I don't know what you're talking about," Lamom said softly, irritated to the breaking point. "Tell me what you want me to do and I'll do it. There's no need to make a fuss."

"Who's fussing?" Nang Lamun demanded, "Who's fussing? I want to commiserate with you about our poverty and you say

I'm fussing? How much more are you going to torment me?"

"I've been thinking all the same," said Lamom, ignoring her mother's reproaches. "Someone like me wouldn't be able to earn a living far from home, so I think I'll take in sewing downstairs. It might be a way to eke things out."

Nang Lamun fell silent when she heard this, although after a pause she went on to say disapprovingly, "You have to invest capital for sewing. Where are you going to get it from?"

"I think I'll buy a machine on hire-purchase, and gradually pay it off. I'll have to get money from you to buy the other odds and ends."

"Hey, what's this? Where am I going to get the money from?" Nang Lamun said, casting an anxious glance at the box at the head of her bed.

"I won't ask for much—two or three hundred should do it," Lamom said to cut the matter short. "I know you've got money put aside, you never spend all the rent you get from the land. You've been saving for a long time. If you want me to help you earn a living, you'd better give me some money."

"Help! I'm fainting!" cried Nang Lamun and threw herself down, but Lamom knew that this was always her mother's escape when defeated by reasoned argument. Usually Lamom would nurse her, but this time she refused to drop the subject they had been discussing. Eventually Nang Lamun had to sit up and get the money to give Lamom as capital for setting up a dressmaking business, all the while delivering a long lecture on the favour she had done her.

From then on, Lamom set up a small dressmaking shop downstairs. Whenever she had time to spare from waiting on her mother, she bent her head to the sewing machine on commissions she had taken on. She had few customers because she did not have enough time to take on much work. Most of her clients were women who lived nearby. One regular customer was a man named Sanit, a clerk in the steam rice mill in that area.

Sanit was a young man, aged between twenty-seven and twenty-eight. He was a solemn bachelor, a man of few words. While not exactly ugly, he was certainly not handsome or dignified. He was of small build, and the marks of the poverty and hardship he had been through showed on his face and skin. Sanit occasionally paid Lamom to sew his singlets and to repair small tears in his shirts and trousers. He was a man of so few words that they did not talk much when he came to the shop, but he always stayed for a long time. Lamom would sit bent over her machine and do other tasks that remained unfinished. She was not garrulous by nature either, and had had so few occasions to speak to anyone that silence had become habitual. The older she grew the less she spoke. After he had visited the shop once, Sanit came more frequently and sat out in the front. In time, Lamom got to know him well enough to learn that he was a bachelor with no immediate family, and that he had had to leave before finishing secondary school to earn his livelihood as a clerk. During this time he had educated himself in his leisure in the hope of finding a better-paid job to establish himself. He had commented to Lamom on the loneliness of being on his own, without a family, but she had remained unmoved because deep down she envied him as someone luckier than she had ever been. She had been so repressed by her mother that she regarded all family ties as burdens to be feared.

Lamom's feelings for Sanit changed gradually. At first she took no notice of him, then her interest grew to the point where she missed him if she did not see him, and, if he was absent for long, worried that he might be ill. If he came to the shop, she was glad and sprightly, and the world seemed a happier place. Her normally impassive face became animated when Sanit talked to her. Often in the afternoon, at the time Sanit usually called, she looked in the mirror to make sure her hair and clothes were in order. Although she did not try to make herself beautiful, she did not want Sanit to see her looking unkempt and dirty. In fact, she showed nearly all the signs of being in love. All that was lacking was her own admission that she loved Sanit and was willing to give herself to him.

Her acquaintance with Sanit, and his periodic visits, made Lamom very happy. It was the first time she had experienced happiness—the happiness that came from knowing someone else in the world was interested in her, the happiness that stemmed from an unselfish and undemanding intimacy. The new relationship also brought her sadness. Once Nang Lamun had been forced to part with the money as capital to earn extra income for her keep, her demands increased. The additional demands were not only for material items, such as the increased amount of liquor she asked Lamom to get and the food she slouched around eating all day, but were also emotional. Every time she saw her—which was almost all day—she would repetitively and endlessly invoke the good she had done for her child, so that at times Lamom, who had endured this all her life, could almost bear it no longer.

When Sanit occasionally came to visit Lamom, at first Nang Lamun did not suspect anything, although every time she heard voices in the room below she would ask who was there and where they had come from. However, when she found that Sanit came regularly and frequently, she made her displeasure clear. Lamom soon found that once Sanit had left, her mother would turn her momentary happiness into torment.

As they were eating, Nang Lamun would say, "My fate, my

karma, is heavier than other people's. I sacrificed my whole life for my beloved daughter, thinking I'd be able to rely on her in my old age, and just look . . . " Here she would wipe away her tears, her fingers still covered in rice and continue, "My daughter's associating with a man—next thing she'll have a husband and leave me all alone. If I weren't old and sick, I wouldn't mind, I'd be able to grit my teeth and bear it, but I'm old and sickly. Am I going to be left to die alone?"

"I don't know what you're talking about. I haven't fallen in love with any man yet!"

"Ungrateful bitch!" Nang Lamun raised her voice. "Do you think you're the only smart one, and that everyone else is blind and deaf? Do you think no-one knows you have a man visiting your room? If you don't love me, so be it, wait and see for yourself. Once you have a fatherless child you'll be crying on my shoulder."

Hurt and resentful, Lamom replied, "Really, Mother, aren't you ashamed of yourself? I told you there's nothing, it's never even occurred to me."

"Thick-skinned! Everybody knows you're thick-skinned, or you wouldn't be running after a man for all to see. I warn you and you've got the nerve to abuse me shamelessly. I never thought I'd give birth to an ogre or a demon, or I wouldn't have wasted my time being pregnant." Having said this, she fell down and rolled around crying, raving on until she finally passed out in an alcoholic stupor.

In fact, had Nang Lamun not shown a disposition to be obstructive or to stop Lamom from seeing Sanit, she might never have felt much towards him. Her mother's selfishness, the obscene language that she went on with every time he came, made her feel that Sanit was her ally against her adversary Nang Lamun. This intimacy, along with other feelings she harboured, soon changed to love, and the more she was reprimanded the stronger her love became.

Had Sanit been bolder, had he declared his love and asked her to elope with him, Lamom would probably have gone immediately, without a second thought. But he was a shy, quiet, serious person, old for his age, and so he did not ask. Lamom knew in her heart that Sanit loved her. Yet when he came he never strayed into the realms of courtship, and talked of ordinary things. Each time he took his leave politely. Lamom was unaware that Sanit thought, as the neighbours did, that she loved her mother more than most people, and would do anything for her. She would not be likely to leave her mother easily, if he asked her to. She might not reject him if he were sufficiently well-off to take her mother in as well, but he was not yet in a position to do so, thus he bided his time.

ONE day Sanit came to see Lamom at home as usual, but as he was leaving he said, "Lamom, I intended to say goodbye to you today."

"Where are you off to, Sanit?" asked Lamom, without looking up from her sewing machine for fear that he would see how much his few words had affected her.

"I'm going to Bangkok," he replied. "There's nothing for me here . . . so I'm going to Bangkok to look around for work—I might get something better than I've got now."

"That's not a bad idea," Lamom said, too confused to think of anything else to say.

"With the knowledge I've acquired I should be able to get something better," Sanit continued. "I thought that . . . when I'm established with a job and a reasonable salary, I'd . . . I'd . . . "

"Say it, Sanit," Lamom thought to herself, her heart pounding as she listened intently. "Say you'll take me to live with you, so I can wait; or if you want me to go with you today or tomorrow, I'll go . . . Say it!" she thought. Without uttering a word her heart beat with increasing rapidity. She was sure that this time Sanit would give voice to her inner thoughts.

But it was not to be. Sanit paused to swallow and summon up his courage, but failed. He finished off the sentence with the meaningless words, "I'd . . . maybe I'd be better off."

That was all. He took his leave. Next morning he set off for Bangkok by boat. All Lamom's hopes and occasional happiness departed with him. At first she cherished the hope that Sanit would send word, but although she waited longingly for news, nothing came. She was unaware that Sanit had sent two letters. But through some quirk of the *karma* of Lamom, of her mother, or of Sanit, the postman delivered each of these, some time apart, when Lamom was busy at the market. Nang Lamun received and read them. Then she hid the letters under the mat beneath the mattress, and did not tell Lamom.

ANOTHER three years passed—three long years for Lamom, in which she aged physically and emotionally; three dry and dessicated years. Lamom had so little hope that she gave up the effort to seek meaning or purpose in life. She lost weight and became thin and emaciated. Although she had never been ill, she looked pale and sickly. She had always looked older than her years, and now acquired the constitution of an older person.

Nang Lamun did not usually let Lamom sweep and clean the area around her bed in the upstairs room. She said she would do it herself, with the result that it was always messy, and offended Lamom's sense of order. Late one morning Nang Lamun went down to have her bath. Lamom happened to go upstairs for something, and seeing her mother's messy bed she changed her mind and went to make it. She pulled the mat up to sweep under it thoroughly for once. Two old letters, the paper yellowing, were placed side by side under the mat. The ink on the envelopes had faded with time, but not so much so that Lamom could not see that they were addressed to her.

She sat down and picked them up out of curiosity. Who could be writing to her, and so long ago—and why had her mother hidden them under the mat? Lamom pulled both letters out at once. Her heart sank when she saw that they were from Sanit. The date on one showed that he had written it after he had been in Bangkok about six months. It was short, as was his style, but its significance for Lamom was enormous.

Dear Lamom,

That day when I took leave of you to come to Bangkok, I intended to tell you that I loved you and wanted to ask you to be my wife, but I wasn't bold enough. I was going to start a new life in Bangkok, and I didn't know whether it'd be better or worse. If I'd spoken then it would have seemed too much, as though I was asking you to risk your life with mine, so I thought I'd wait and see how I went first.

I'm now working with a firm in Bangkok. My salary is higher than it was, enough for two people—you and me—to live on comfortably, and there are prospects for the future. I beg you to come and share my life. I don't want to say too much, as we've known each other long enough to know how we feel. If you believe I can make you happy, and decide to live with me, please write to me at the above address. I'll wait every day for your reply.

Missing you terribly,
Sanit

The other letter, written six months after the first, was shorter, and did not refer to the previous one. It was simply to let Lamom know that he was married and had a family in Bangkok.

Lamom sat rooted to the spot. Her senses were numb, as if someone had smashed a heavy object on her brain. Behind her, Nang Lamun came wheezing slowly up the stairs. Lamom sat immobile and did not look around. Her flesh crept as she thought how her own mother was her worst enemy, the person who had squeezed and trampled her feelings throughout her life and had destroyed all her chances of normal happiness.

"What are you doing, Lamom?" Nang Lamun said loudly, almost shouting, when she saw her daughter sitting staring at the two letters. She walked over quickly, wheezing loudly, her whole body rippling. Seeing that her daughter sat still, not speaking or turning around, she called out, "Help, I'm tired, I'm fainting!" and fell to the ground for Lamom to rush over and assist.

But Lamom sat where she was, not moving a muscle, her eyes fixed on the two letters in front of her. When Nang Lamun saw that her daughter was ignoring her, she revived from her 'faint' herself. She stayed where she was, near Lamom, and burst into floods of tears while starting to harp on her munificence and self-sacrifice in the old words and phrases Lamom had had to listen to for so long.

The sound of her mother's sobs, her incessant aggrieved, selfish rantings, starting softly but building up to a pitch, worked on Lamom as if a thread or a wire had been strung through her for a long, long time. The wire had been pulled more and more taut until finally it snapped with a massive spring. Lamom grabbed a pillow that was lying at hand and pressed it on her mother's face. She pushed it down, down. She would face the consequences, all she asked was that she would never again have to hear the voice, to hear the words she had heard all her life. The noise stopped abruptly. Nang Lamun thrashed about for a moment but Lamom kept pushing the pillow with a strength she would not have believed possible. After a long time, she relaxed her efforts and drew away. She sat gasping with exhaustion, then gradually lifted the pillow. Nang Lamun was dead.

Lamom sat until she felt rested, then made the bed. She used all her remaining energy to drag her mother's body on to the bed, and covered it with a cloth. She walked downstairs as if in a dream. Her old life had ended with her mother's death. She could not say how her new life would turn out. The thought that she had committed the most serious of all crimes, matricide, did not enter her head. She felt only relief, as if she had got rid of a parasite that had been sucking her life blood.

WHEN Lamom told the neighbours that her mother had died in a fainting fit they believed her, and out of pity offered her various kinds of assistance. After she had arranged for her mother's funeral in the traditional way, she sold the shophouse, which gave her enough to live on for the next few months. Then she packed her few possessions into a trunk and took the boat from Ban Phaen to Bangkok.

As the boat steered through the storm Lamom sat looking into the darkness with an empty heart. In her past life she had known nothing but emptiness; the future seemed to hold nothing but more emptiness. True, she intended to visit Sanit in Bangkok, but what would he have to give her now that he had a wife?

Who could judge whether it was merit or *karma* for Lamom when the boat overturned, plunging the emptiness of her past, present and future from sight, to disappear amidst the sounds of the pounding rain and the awesome fury of the storm raging in the darkness.

NORI—THE WRITER

NORI came from Wisetchaichan district. His mother had told him he was called Nori because he had been talkative and full of blandishments since he was little. He was the youngest son of a well-off local family. Nori understood from his earliest years that they owed their prosperity to the inheritance of his mother, Nang Num, and were maintained by the industry and effort of that same person. Nai Som, his father, was generally regarded as a drunkard. He did no regular work, and left it to his wife to support the family on her own.

Nori had never seen his father parted from a bottle and a small glass, as far back as he could remember. No matter where he sat, the bottle and glass were by his side, as if they constituted one of life's absolute necessities. Once when Nai Som was not looking, Nori poured some of the liquid from the bottle into the glass to taste, but he had had to spit it out immediately. Instead of the delicious sweet flavour he had expected, the liquid had an acid taste and made his mouth pucker. He could not swallow it.

But the strange taste of the bottled liquid gave Nori a new interest in watching his father drink. He tried to observe the effects of alcohol. Some days he sat at a distance and watched his father drink and talk noisily with his cronies, ending up boasting and blustering or quarreling and coming to blows. Sometimes no-one came, and his father sat drinking alone. The more he drank the more bizarre his behaviour. When there was no-one else to talk to or fight with, he turned to Nori's mother. First he criticized whatever she was doing, then cursed and swore at her. If, occasionally, she argued, he hit her violently. Nori sneaked into his room or hid behind one of the pillars for fear that a few of the blows might fall his way. Whether Nai Som fought with his friends or his wife, ultimately he was always the loser—not to friends or wife, but to the liquor in the bottle. He rampaged until he passed out, senseless, on the veranda and his wife half-carried, half-dragged him onto the bed. Then peace reigned in the house and everyone slept undisturbed. Nori sometimes woke suddenly in the night to hear his father pouring liquid into a glass and drinking it loudly and thirstily. He lay listening to the sound in the dark.

At times, when his father had ranted until he passed out, his mother hugged Nori, her youngest, closely to her. Crying, she told him her troubles as if he were a mature adult. She talked of when his father was young and strong, with the will and energy to look after his wife and children as others did. Then he drank only occasionally, not incessantly as he did now.

"I never thought," Nang Num sobbed, "I never thought your father would get this bad. When we were first married he was fine. He worked harder than anyone. So I thought I'd put my life in his hands. Then his friends—first this one, then that one —urged him away. Sometimes they'd come and drink here; sometimes they'd go elsewhere. I never interfered. I thought he'd be able to look after himself. First he drank only in company, but then he started to drink alone. In the beginning he drank only in the late afternoon and evening, then it got so he drank from morning well into the night. He has to have a drink as soon as he wakes. Listen to this, Nori! Now nearly all his old friends avoid him; none of the neighbours would look twice at him. I have to earn enough to feed you from day to day. And if I didn't, what would you eat? Then when I leave the house he accuses me of deserting him! When I come back he abuses me. If I don't go, he accuses me of laziness and says I only sit around eating, and curses and beats me again . . . Take heed! You've watched me suffer, so remember never to touch a drop when you grow up. Your father's lost to us already, I don't want my child to follow him."

Nori only understood part of what his mother said, but he took in the tears and sobs of suffering, born of hurt and disappointment. The things he saw and felt made Nori deeply sorry for his mother. He thought then, as a child would, that if drink could cause his mother such suffering, he would never touch it.

Even though alcohol made Nai Som disagreeable, one aspect of his nature did no harm to anyone. He liked to read and collect books. These ranged from the dynastic sagas that used to be available for a few *satang*, to sermons, epic poems, and improvised theatrical dialogue. Before Nori could read for himself, Nai Som read these books to him around midday, loudly, with the proper rhyme and rhythm. Nori listened at leisure until he dropped off. Som's love of books and reading made Nori familiar with books from childhood. He regarded them as a means of soothing the feelings and as good, trustworthy friends, because his father was always better tempered when he read, and did not get wild or angry or scold his wife and son at all.

When Nori was a bit older, his mother entrusted him to *Luang Ta* (reverend grandfather) at the temple so that he could learn to read after the monks had eaten their midday meal.* Nori was soon able to read, because he was already familiar with books and was not lazy or scared of learning. From then on, whenever he had a spare moment, his father called on Nori to read to him. He read through all of his father's books, then began on another round, until eventually he knew them by heart. He could recite long passages of their narrative and poems, but he did not tire of them. The letters printed neatly on the page seemed pleasantly ordered and the rhythm and beat of the books lulled him into happiness.

His early love of books kept Nori at home. He did not run around much outside or in the paddy fields with his cousins or other children. He stayed with the abbot at the temple long enough to read and write well. One holy day as his mother was presenting the meal to the abbot he remarked, "Your youngest is a clever boy. I've taught a lot of pupils, but none who learned as quickly as he. It'd be good if you could send him to school for further studies."

"I hadn't planned for him to go so far," his mother replied. "I only thought I'd send him to you until he could read and write, so we'd be able to use his help about the place."

"You've got other children," the abbot said. "Nori's elder siblings are old enough to do a bit of work. Couldn't you let Nori off, to make a career through books—you'll be able to rely on him in your old age if he gets on in government service and becomes a person of high rank."

Nori's mother reflected on what the abbot had said. Shortly after, she sent him to live with relatives in Ayutthaya to embark on and complete his schooling.

---

* It was traditional for boys to learn to read and write at schools in the village temples.

Nori's time in Ayutthaya was one of the most important periods in his life. He started school, and in the higher grades he learnt about Thai history. He was excited by the discovery of history. The events he read of in the Ayutthayan chronicles stimulated him. Before he had read only cheap romantic fiction. He had tried to imagine the characters in them as flesh and blood, with little success. The characters and scenes in the books were too far from reality as he knew it.

When he came to live in the provincial centre of Ayutthaya, amidst the ruins which testified to the brilliance of the former royal capital, and read the chronicles which mentioned temples and landmarks in districts he passed every day, Nori's absorption grew. The characters took on flesh and blood and came to life in his imagination. The more he devoured those books, the more he conjured up the disposition of those who were once the main players in the Ayutthayan kingdom, and the more he fell to daydreaming. He reflected on the struggles and conflicts; on love, jealousy, and revenge; he thought of events replete with glorious sacrifice. He basked happily in the glow of victory, and was dashed by darkest defeat. Out of school, he wandered around the various places mentioned in the chronicles. He visited old palaces and ruined temples, and gazed on the remains of forts and city gates.

Sometimes he stretched out on the lawn in front of the Mongkhonbophit temple and let his imagination drift with the stories he had read with such intensity. Looking ahead using his imagination and emotions, he saw the Ayutthayan chronicles, of which he felt he was custodian, pass by at close quarters... King U Thong, who had built the city with such hopes and splendid dreams . . . King Ai Phraya and Yi Phraya fighting on elephant back at Mahatat temple, just nearby . . . The Thammathian rebels advancing on the palace—closer—the sound of

gunshot—Thammathian falling from the elephant's neck . . .
people panicking, scattering in all directions. Nori saw all this
clearly, as if he were standing there watching.

He was not interested in whether others shared his feelings,
or had the same insights, and he was not concerned that his
special talent of imaginative reconstruction was a rare gift. If
he had known from the outset that these phenomena were a
writer's special endowment, and that they would bring trouble
every now and again because of his inability to adjust the
vastness of his imagination to the level of ordinary life, he
might have thrown off these pleasing thoughts as though
they burned, or were harmful and repugnant, and set about
becoming familiar with mundane things. He would have
anchored his spirit to a crude and secure base in life, that is, the
pursuit of money and profit to satisfy coarse and basic physical
wants. Had Nori done that, his life might have been different,
and he might have enjoyed the happiness most people desire.
But perhaps all the elements that combined to produce Nori
were too delicate. For whatever reason, he let himself drift into
a state of strange colour and glowing light, devoid of anything
of substance to cling to. Nori found happiness in his dreams,
but sometimes those very dreams created intolerable heartache
and suffering. Even though his dreams were sad and bitter-
sweet, he felt complete and incomparable satisfaction in such
sorrow.

Nori's maturity increased with every passing day. The
knowledge he had gained from the provincial school was
second to none. And in subjects such as composition, the
teacher always specially commended him, so that he gained a
reputation for being good at Thai. He put special effort into
the newspaper he and his friends helped to produce in class.
Even though he was old enough to know that their newspaper

was a game, not real, he still thought it was very important. He was proud that his friends had honoured him by making him editor, and did all he could to make the handwritten paper worth reading. One day the teacher picked up a copy and read it, and called Nori in the next day after school to say, "Nori, did you produce this magazine?"

"Yes," Nori replied awkwardly, not knowing how the teacher would react.

"I'm not criticizing you," he smiled. "If producing this doesn't interfere with your schoolwork, I'm all for it, because you're using your brains. Better than getting up to other mischief."

The teacher picked up the magazine and flicked through the pages, opening it at the page with one of Nori's stories under the pen-name 'Nok Salika' (myna bird) and said, "Didn't you write this?"

"Yes," said Nori again. He thought that because his story was about love and romance between a young couple, as was then fashionable, he might be warned not to write like that again. But instead the teacher said,

"You write well, Nori. Even I liked it. Your writing is very mature. But I want to give you some advice."

He put the volume down, and gazed unseeingly ahead.

"Once, when I was young, I used to like this kind of thing… but writing isn't a real profession in this country. I used to write novels in Bangkok, but then I had to return home. I came to teach here because I couldn't stand the privations. I want to warn you, because I don't want you to try. I'm worried that you'll suffer the hardship I once did."

That was all he said before letting Nori go home. But his well-intentioned words had no lasting effect on Nori, who still regarded writing as a game, not serious, at that stage. Deep down, he believed that books were not dangerous but more enlivening than any other thing. He had not yet seen the difficulties which his teacher claimed to have experienced.

Nori's father died only a few months before the end of the school year. So it was that as soon as his final examinations were over, he hurried home for his father's cremation. His mother had kept the body until he returned to undertake the ceremony. He still remembered, clearly, how cruelly his father had treated his mother under the influence of alcohol; but he was moved to see her grief on his father's death. As she cried, she said to him, "Your father shouldn't have died so soon, Nori. Drink shortened his life. Without it he'd still be here, hale and hearty —but he drank till he was a shadow of his former self. His mind wandered, and people thought he was mad. He died of alcoholism. Again and again I begged him to give it up. If he'd been able to, he'd probably be with us still."

His mother began to sob again, out of sorrow and regret for the life of the one she had loved, needlessly wasted through his own weakness and lack of self-control.

After the cremation, Nori stayed at home as a gentleman of leisure. Neither his mother, nor anyone else in his family, asked him to till the fields or do any of the other heavy tasks that everyone else did as a matter of course. They respected him as a scholar, who had mastered higher levels of learning right up to graduation from the government high school. Nori, with his knowledge and learning, seemed remote from hard manual labour. Everyone was content to continue with their own heavy work, and to let him enjoy the fruits of their labour for nothing, out of respect. Every time he expressed a wish to help with anything to do with the house, his mother said, "Don't worry, Nori. Do you think you'd be able to manage heavy lifting and carrying with your education? Your type is better suited to being a teacher or an official."

Because they all shared her view, no-one raised any objection when he announced one day that he was going to look for work in Bangkok, to get on in life. Everybody agreed that it would be a good thing because they all hoped he might some day become a high-ranking official, so that his relatives could bask in his reflected glory and fall back on him for support. His mother immediately found some money for him, and gave him the address of a relative in Bangkok he could stay with.

The night before he left for Bangkok, his mother called him into her room for a long lecture on the evils of alcohol and intoxicants. She used his father's story to illustrate for Nori once again how drink could destroy a person's basic goodness, and ultimately even life itself. She cried as she spoke, from anxiety that far from home and its restraining influence he might be tempted by vice. At the end she took a small amulet from a box and told him it was for his protection. But before she handed it over, she made him swear before that image that he would never touch alcohol. Then she let him put the amulet round his neck, as a reminder to uphold the oath he had made before the sacred image to the one who had given him birth.

Nori took the oath that night willingly, in all innocence. He could see the dangers of drink, and had never had the slightest desire to touch a drop.

Next day, Nori sailed expectantly to Bangkok. Bangkok… the great city, gateway to a brilliant life of fame, honour, and abiding values. He was well aware that he had no more to offer than anyone else, apart from his intention to do well in the life he had often dreamt about through his emotions and the special gifts of the dreamer. The beauty of his dream was beyond the imaginative capacity of most ordinary people. As long as that charmed life continued to beckon from the end of the road, he would struggle towards it. He told himself frankly at the outset that it did not matter if he could not reach his destination; the journey itself, as he drew nearer, was enjoyment enough. If he had been able to tell a seer about his dreams and destiny, he would have been told at once that he was over-ambitious. But he told nobody. Thus he was unaware that the brilliant life he had painted for himself was far removed from reality, and that the path of ambition was marked by pitfalls. Yet had someone been able to tell him, the knowledge would not have hindered his dreams. Dreaming was his destiny.

Nori's relatives in Bangkok knew a senior official, of the rank of *phraya.** A few days after he arrived he was put into this person's care. He was to stay in the *phraya's* house and be of service to him. In return, Nori was placed as a clerk in the branch of the division which he headed.

The next two or three years in the city were a time of consolidation for Nori. He observed life in Bangkok and etched it into his memory. He recorded facts and emotions produced by force of circumstance. This may have been why the work assigned to him did not proceed as he intended. His official duties seemed dry, colourless, and devoid of soul, down to every last word on the file. Nori wanted life, movement— colours which reflected in sunlight, wind that tossed the branches, joy and sorrow, tears and laughter. These qualities were not easy to find in the atmosphere of the civil service.

But life in the official's house where Nori stayed turned out to be much livelier than he had imagined. True, it was not his life. He was just a retainer. Like an insect or a beetle, he looked up from the ground to the flowers open to the wind

* A non-hereditary title bestowed on the second-highest-ranking government official used before the change to constitutional monarchy in 1932.

and sun, as birds and butterflies flew around and paused in greeting. The glamorous lives of the rich and famous were free of obstacles. There was no hindrance to arranging for life to be forever pleasant and beautiful, with delicious food and dazzling ornaments. Voices resonant with good breeding, laughter purposefully cultivated to sound musical, reached his ears from a distance. He drank in all that he saw and heard as if his heart were a canvas on which a clever artist had drawn, then coloured into an attractive picture. Sometimes he dreamt about it, and in his dreams he was surrounded by that life of luxury, as its very centre.

His boss and patron, *Chaokhun*,* had many daughters. But the one whom everyone called 'Khun Lek' meant most to Nori. She was about his age, and was the most beautiful woman he had ever met in his young life. Thus it was natural that after he met her, she too became part of his dream. And because she was unassuming, and happy to talk to Nori—one of her father's retinue—as an equal without making him feel inferior, he worshipped her as his personal goddess. He dreamed incessantly of the day he would be sufficiently exalted to speak to Khun Lek as a lover. Life would only be fulfilled when he held her to him. He would want nothing more.

Khun Lek shared his love of reading. She often passed on books she had read. When he had finished, they discussed the book—its plot, characters, and author. She talked about books at length, especially to a listener as familiar with them as Nori. Khun Lek never seemed to tire, and it was a chance for him to spend a longish time with her every day. She sat on the stone steps at the back of the house, and Nori sat a suitable distance away on a lower step. He gazed into her face, and concentrated

* An informal term used to address a *phraya*.

his love on it. That was his happiest time, a time of hopes and desires, and his life's dream seemed to be floating within reach. But the most important day in his life came when she said, bright-eyed, out of the blue, "Nori, do you know . . . if I could choose . . . a lover I could give my whole life to . . . it would have to be a man who could write. He would have to be a writer who could soothe me to contentment. His writings would have to elevate the ordinary reader, including me, to a new life, removed from the monotony of the daily round. He could be poor. Nori . . . he could even be ugly . . . but the words that flowed from his pen would have to be sweet yet strong. He would have to mingle sugar with poison in his speech. And when I meet someone like that . . . then . . . "

Khun Lek left the sentence unfinished for Nori to round off. He understood her well, but he did not understand that she spoke in the height of emotion, under the sway of a book she had just finished. She spoke like the heroine in the novel, who willingly sacrificed her life of glamour for a young writer who aimed to bring about social revolution. She spoke because she wanted to hear those moving words emanate from her own lips. There was no more to it than that, and having spoken, Khun Lek promptly forgot and did not hark back to reflect on the matter again.

But her words had a dramatic effect on Nori, causing him to take a new turning and changing him into an author. From that day on Nori began to write. He used the time when he should have been sleeping to draw upon his dreams and innermost thoughts, commiting them meticulously to paper. His first story was the diary of a young and unfortunate man, a poor man who had fallen in love with a woman of higher status. His love was thus out of reach. He barely had to think as he wrote. All his feelings, his emotions, his dreams, poured into words as if possessed by a force of their own. He merely held the pen, and it would begin to write and write, like a living, moving creature. Nori wanted his first piece to be a tribute to his love for Khun Lek, so he gave it to her the morning after he finished it and left for work in a state of suspense.

When he returned that afternoon, Khun Lek hurried down to meet him at the back of the house. She handed back his story, and said excitedly, "Nori! I never thought you could write so well. I read it in one go! I really couldn't put it down! I'll tell you unashamedly that I had to cry in parts. I don't know where you managed to find such moving words. I like your story very much. It's a lot better than some of the ones that get published, even if it is only your first. You should try and get it published too. Then—who knows—you might become famous, and I'll be very proud of having been first to read your stories."

Her words were like water nurturing fertile ground where seeds lay dormant, causing them to swell and burst into life. She spoke excitedly, with flushed cheeks and sparkling eyes, almost melting his heart with her beauty. She laughed softly and turned back to the house, saying she had things to do. Nori returned slowly to his room, brimming over with happiness and joy.

A few days later Nori presented himself in front of the editor of one of the newspapers. The editor looked up at him and said, "What do you want?"

"I . . . I," Nori could barely speak from nervousness. "I've written a story—I'd like you to publish it—if you think it's suitable." Nori handed his manuscript to the editor with a trembling hand.

The editor took it and flipped through, then said,

"By Salika Kaeo (gem myna bird). Hmm! That sounds good. Is your name Salika?"

"No, my name is Nori. Salika is my pen-name."

"I see. It sounds good anyway," said the editor. "How about this. I'll take your story, and if it's any good, I'll publish it." As he said this he put it into a tray beside him.

"And . . . um . . . when will I know?" Nori asked.

The editor looked at him and said, "Hmm, I don't really know . . . Come back and see in four or five days."

The next four or five days seemed to pass more slowly than time ever had before. He thought only of his manuscript, and of when he would find out what had happened to it. Maybe the editor would look at him with the same excitement as Khun Lek had, and his story would be printed in the paper. But maybe the editor would hand the story back, telling him it did not quite meet their standard. Nori was restless for days. He barely ate or slept, and on the fifth day he presented himself at the editor's desk again.

The editor looked up from his writing and asked, "What do you want?"

"I . . . I . . . gave you a story to consider." Nori was so nervous he could barely get the words out.

"Ah! What was it and where is it?" asked the editor, stretching out his hand.

Nori's heart sank. No-one had paid any attention to his carefully constructed story. The editor could not even remember receiving it.

"No," he said in a barely audible voice, "I've given it to you. You said to come back again in four or five days."

The editor looked at him in puzzlement. Then his face lit up as he remembered, and he said, leafing through his tray of papers, "Ah! That's right. Your story was by a parrot or a talking myna or something, wasn't it?"

Nori saw his manuscript sitting in the same place as he

had last seen it. It showed no signs of having been touched. The editor picked it up and flicked through it, then said with concern, "It's still a bit weak, and you're a new author. Try improving it, then come back again." The editor bent back over his work, to show that the encounter was over.

Nori slowly descended the staircase. His hopes and dreams were shattered. Those few words—'still a bit weak—you're a new author'—echoed in his ears. A huge gate seemed to bar the way and to stand between him and the pathway to his magnifi-cent future. 'Still a bit weak'—that must have been an easy explanation, because how could the editor know if he had not read it? But 'you're a new author' was a formidable reason. Being a newcomer to the writer's circle was a significant obstacle. How could he wipe out his newness if the newness itself was a hindrance from the outset?

Someone coming up the stairs banged into him with such force that he swayed against the wall. The other person, who turned out to be a man, looked as though he were about to fall down the stairs, so Nori quickly reached out to grab him by the arm. The man swayed over on to Nori, reeking of alcohol. The drunk said brokenly, "Thanks a lot. Thanks. Truly thanks. If your excellency hadn't saved my life, I would have fallen down-tairs. No! Fallen down the steers—no, that's not it— fallen, fallen down the—let it be, down those things that are in steps, and died. Thank you very much your excellency—I'll have to buy you a few drinks for this!"

"It doesn't matter," Nori said as he tried to loosen the hands that held both his arms in a tight grip. But the hands squeezed even more tightly and would not let go. The owner of the hands yelled out, "Hey! It does matter! How can it not matter! I'm Nai Chuang Chomphusot, a man of gratitude. Peole who save lives have to be repaid—I've repaid many—people are often saving me, so I keep repaying—I'm Chuang Chomphu-sot, the famous author. 'Phaya Nak' (serpent king) is the pen-name for the tales of passion, hot and spicy; 'Kon Khop' (red-tailed pipe snake) for the cute pieces; 'Pi Kaeo' (ashy kukri snake) for love stories. All the same person. All the pen-names are to do with snakes, because I was born in the year of the snake. My father said it was the year of the dragon. My mother argued that it was the year of the snake. Dragon or snake, it doesn't matter, there are plenty of readers—first-class writer—" Nai Chuang reached over and leant on Nori's shoulder, dropped his head, and fell asleep.

Nori stood rigid, his hair standing on end as if under a spell. He had read all of these pen-names—Phaya Nak, Kon Khop, Pi Kaeo—they were famous, everyone had heard of them. Stories by Phaya Nak he had read with violent feelings, his emotions boiling over with indignation at various social injustices. He had read the bits and pieces by Kon Khop in a humorous mood. The more he read of them, the more he saw the importance of the little things around him, which gave pleasure to ordinary life. And as for the love stories of Pi Kaeo . . . who had not read them? Nori had immersed himself in the sweetness of love in the stories by Pi Kaeo, and felt he had never encountered a truer love than that he found in the pages of books. Sometimes Pi Kaeo's prose made his heart ache so much he could hardly bear it. He had not known that all three pen-names belonged to the same person—this scruffy, alcohol-drenched drunk standing slumped before him, half asleep. Nori was not sure he was telling the truth. He might have been boasting under the influence of drink. But there was something about him—some of his words, his actions, and even his ageless face, neither old nor young—that made Nori hesitate to refuse him outright.

He tried to extricate himself but when he moved, Nai Chuang, the famous writer, woke up and said, "Wait a minute —wait a minute—don't escape. Let's go upstairs together. I have to drop off a manuscript. Then we can have a chat and a drink—What's your name?"

"Nori."

"Aha! Nori! That's a good name, I'll have to remember it. I'll call one of my heroes Nori."

Saying this, Nai Chuang half-pulled, half-dragged Nori back to the top floor of the newspaper office. Nori's doubts vanished as the editor and others welcomed Nai Chuang. The editor got up from his desk and greeted him warmly, extending both hands to take the manuscript, written on a stack of worn old paper, as though it were highly valuable. He said, "*Khru* (teacher)! You came just at the right moment! I was waiting for your manuscript. I thought you weren't coming."

"Hey! When I say I'll come, I come. Have you got the money ready? I'm going to have to take my mate out—see, my old mate Nori, I owe him a lot," Chuang said, slapping Nori on the back as if to introduce him to everyone seated there.

The editor quickly returned to his desk and put some money in an envelope which he gave to Khru Chuang, then turned and smiled at Nori and said, "I . . . didn't know that you knew Khru Chuang."

"I . . . " Nori meant to explain that he had only just met him as he was going downstairs, but Khru Chuang interrupted, "We've known each other for ages—you could say we were old mates." He turned to Nori and said, as if to explain, "Time isn't important. Friendship is above time. For true friends, knowing each other for a day is the same as twenty years."

He took the money from the editor, put his arm through Nori's, and led him downstairs and across the road to a liquor shop opposite the printing house. Khru Chuang ordered a drink, and tried to persuade Nori to have one with him. He did not mind when Nori firmly refused. Chuang drank, and got Nori to talk about himself, to the point where he confessed that he was becoming a writer and wanted to sit at Chuang's feet. Khru Chuang accepted him readily, and explained that as Nori was about to enter the book world, he would need someone to make introductions and open doors. Khru Chuang said he would do this for Nori, but he also said, "We mustn't lose touch. Visit often, so we can easily help each other. You saved my life; I'll help you till the end of yours." Khru Chuang drew a finger dipped in whisky across Nori's throat, then his own, as a symbol of their enduring friendship.

That day Nori returned home contented. Even though his work had not been published and read yet, he had met an important person in whom he had been interested for a long time, and that person had been extremely friendly. Nori felt as though he had stepped into another world, beyond that of ordinary people—a dream world, wherein words glittered like precious gems. Superficially, Khru Chuang was a scruffy drunkard; but the more Nori listened to him, the more he felt that he possessed an eternal flame which shone radiantly through the tattered coverings. Nori was drawn to Khru Chuang within a few hours, because he knew that a flame of the same light and colour smouldered deep down within himself.

OVER the next two years, people began to hear of the pen-name Salika Kaeo. Khru Chuang helped him get his stories published in various magazines. At that time there was no remuneration for stories published in magazines by new writers, but seeing an important part of oneself in print was a reward in itself. Nori still remembered how he had read his first published story over and over, as if it was written in words from heaven. He felt replete with happiness every time he read it. He also remembered Khun Lek's sparkling eyes as she had looked at him with respect and excitement when his first story was published. Then, and subsequently, she had spoken to him in a voice full of hidden meanings which inspired hope and fresh dreams.

The benefits of his relationship with Khru Chuang were incalculable. His words and opinions were like small tongues of fire that kindled an incandescent flame within Nori's breast. Sometimes a single sentence of Chuang's would enable him to come back and write a whole story. Khru Chuang exerted an uncanny influence on him, and it was because of this that Nori sought opportunities to meet him nearly every day.

But the one thing about associating with Khru Chuang which discomforted Nori most of all was the matter of alcohol. As Chuang drank all day, naturally everyone who came to see him had to resign themselves to becoming his regular drinking partners. Nori could deduce this because he was accustomed from childhood to other people's drinking habits, having had an alcoholic for a father. Likewise, Chuang and his friends always invited him to join them in a drink whenever they met, but he turned them down, because the amulet his mother had given him when he left home still hung around his neck as witness to the promise he had made her, and her exhortations against drink still rang in his ears. Yet, even though he stuck by his refusal to touch alcohol because of his vow, the refusal always made him feel an outsider, not sharing the intimate world and habits of the mentor he so venerated.

One day the opportunity for resounding fame in the book world arrived. That afternoon Nori accompanied Khru

Chuang to the newspaper office that Nori had first contacted. Chuang always took Nori to the publishing houses with him on principle, to get to know people. He arrived just as everyone had finished work. The editor broke out a bottle, and they sat and talked. At one point the editor said, "Khru, the long story I've been running in the paper is nearly finished. Have you got any others salted away?"

"No, I haven't," said Khru Chuang.

"Then you'd better write a new one," the editor suggested.

"You know me," said Khru Chuang. "I could write a new one. But if I can't keep the instalments going, you and I will fall out over nothing."

The editor reflected, "If you don't write, who should we get? A long story with daily instalments can't afford to have interruptions."

Nori had not paid much attention, and started sharply when he heard Khru Chuang say, "Let Nori try his hand. He's becoming quite well known nowadays, too."

"But . . . ," Nori said, opening his mouth to protest that he was not quite up to it yet, but Khru Chuang got in first and said, "Come on! No matter, I'll help. In fact I'm scared everybody is going to fall for you!"

"I don't know what I'm supposed to write," Nori said.

"It's dead easy," Khru Chuang replied. "Right now, people like reading excerpts from the Chinese chronicles. Nearly all the papers are running them. You can try a new tack—write chronicles, but make it Thai chronicles. What do you say to that?" he turned to ask the editor.

"Sounds all right. If Nori agrees to write, I'll publish it."

Nori knew at once that he could follow the line Khru Chuang had suggested, and could do it well. All he needed was for someone to suggest an idea and in a flash the way ahead was clear. His fingers tapped lightly on the table. He could see it all clearly. He heard Chuang saying, "Sure, he'll write it, but you can't just publish it for nothing. There has to be some return. A novel takes a bit of effort."

"Okay," the editor said, "but what should we agree on?"

"Well, what say you pay him as much as you're paying me."

FROM then on, Nori began to write in earnest. He wrote stories based on the Thai chronicles, as Chuang had suggested, reliving to the full the dreams and emotions of his student days in Ayutthaya. He wrote from the heart, using every nerve. The letters flowed effortlessly from pen to paper, with no need for time or thought. They were like caged birds, flying swiftly and joyously away at the opportunity for freedom. Key characters in the chronicles came back to life. Whenever he thought of someone, he found them at his elbow, whispering the details of their lives and thoughts and feelings into his ear. He took it all down. The countryside and changing seasons appeared before him, and he described each scene as vividly as though he had seen it with his own eyes. Whatever his dreams, hopes and wishes they were all recorded. His flaming passion for Khun Lek enabled him to depict love in a new light; his ability to observe life's complexities allowed him to embroider his chronicle in a strange and compelling way; his gregariousness (for which he was named Nori) made his words come to life, so that his dialogue flowed with the rhythms of speech itself rather than the dead, hard language of prose.

Before long, his stories had taken off like wildfire. His pen-name was on everyone's lips. His earnings did not amount to much, but were enough to live on without a clerical job. Yet he did not give up his work, because he was still staying in the *chaokhun*'s house. Lek's presence was the magnet which kept him there. As his fame exploded like fireworks in literary circles, the way Lek spoke to and looked at him led Nori to believe that their relationship would soon reach its culmination. So one day when Chuang said to him, "You know something Nori? You've made it. That last story was very moving. I raise the white flag of surrender, and I do it gladly, because I love you dearly. Young Nori, you'd have to be the best writer of our time—it'd be difficult to find any others as good."

Nori only laughed, knowing Khru Chuang's ignorance of his real goal.

In the end, it was Lek's betrothal to the son of a well-to-do family, arranged by the *chaokhun* himself, which dealt an irrevocable blow to all Nori's rising hopes and aspirations. He did not say a word to anyone when he found out, or display any untoward emotion for others to see. He walked slowly to his room and packed his belongings into a chest. That night, he escaped and fled the *chaokhun*'s house without a word of farewell. He intended to embark on a new path, and did not want to encounter old experiences. Khru Chuang welcomed him warmly for the night. And when Khru Chuang could not console Nori, he offered him a drink. That night, Nori broke his vow to his mother and began drinking with Khru Chuang.

He poured his heart out as he drank. Unable to comfort him by any other means, Khru Chuang filled his glass with the best of intentions. Nori kept drinking, unbearably oppressed by his fate. Eventually he fell into a drunken slumber for the first time in his life.

He woke at dawn, with the sensation of someone bashing his heart till it ached. If he so much as moved, coughed, or sneezed, the pain shot to his head as though he had been pierced with a sword blade or a spear. He lay staring up at the yellow roof, but no, it was not only the roof, everything was yellow—the mattress, the mosquito net, and the sky he glimpsed through the window. He kept his thoughts to himself, because his throat felt hot and dry, as if someone had been fanning the flames in it all night. Carefully, he eased himself into a sitting position and put his hand to his head, and groaned softly in excruciating pain. He sat like that for a long time, eyes fixed on his chest.

After a while he noticed a small amulet around his neck. That was right! His mother had given him the amulet to remind him of his vow to abstain from alcohol. Nori was horrified as he remembered how he had broken his vow to his mother, taken before this amulet. Would he now face danger and ill fortune as declared in the oath he had sworn? But no—fate, unpropitious and unsought, had touched him before he had broken his word —since the day when the woman he adored and worshipped, the cornerstone of all his aspirations, was lost irrevocably to another. This twist of fate had struck him down even before the breaking of his oath—so why should he fear the consequences now? Anyway, he had broken it, all of it. Nothing was left, and nothing could be revoked. His good deeds had produced nothing—he might as well experiment with some bad ones, now he was a worthless, dishonourable person whom nobody wanted. "What was that?" Nori asked himself, "Ah, the amulet mother gave me still hangs round my neck, still moves with my body, as a reminder of my oath, and my resolve always to do the right thing." He reached out and removed the amulet from his neck and placed it by the bedhead. He would be pleased if the thin gold chain from which it hung tempted someone to come and remove it. He never wanted to see it again.

THREE years later, his fame had spread throughout the literary world. His pen was still sharp and passionate; his fans were increasingly enthusiastic, and there were more of them. Before, love and dreams had driven his spirited writing. But now they had evaporated he was able to write, and write racily to the public's taste, because of alcohol alone. Drink was his only comfort—his true friend, the inspiration which drove his pen. Nowadays, he had to drink before he could write, or his mind would cloud over and his wits desert him. But no sooner had the contents of a glass of alcohol touched his throat, then everything became clear and he could draw a vivid and compelling pen picture of his world and how he thought it should be. This had little meaning, however. Another glass, and as likely as not he would overturn his heaven and create hell instead. On paper, he created different individuals, diverse and colourful, who displayed their characteristics in varying degrees of vice and virtue. After a few drinks, he was Brahma the creator, himself creating humanity. He could make people as beautiful, as ugly, as fearsome, as he wished, as high-minded or as base and vile. Retribution for the actions of all these different individuals was in his hands alone. Brahma-like, they did not matter to him—he was their creator, with powers of life and death over them. Writing was enjoyable. The whole of the past was swallowed up in a glass of alcohol. Sometimes he laughed so loudly his small rented room seemed about to collapse around his ears. Sometimes he sobbed as he wrote, his face bathed in tears. At times he gritted his teeth and ripped his pen across the page like the sharp, cutting sword of the executioner, able to cut life short at a single blow.

Nori must have inherited many of his father's characteristics, because once he began to drink he took to it wholeheartedly, like a duck to water. He could drink day and night, and never have enough. Even his drinking friends and acquaintances looked on in amazement. Like his father, he could drink more than others, so alcohol consumed and destroyed him all the faster.

TWO years later, his physical appearance was unrecognizable. Dirty and scruffy, his clothes torn through neglect and poverty, he was skinny, with thinning hair and hollow, shadow-ringed eyes. Although he was thin, his skin was taut and puffy, as if from retention of water between skin and bone.

Worst of all, he could no longer write. Deprived of alcohol, he lacked the strength to hold pen or paper. And after swigging half a glass, he was too drunk even to see the letters clearly. He was in terrible straits. Indifferent to food, his only problem now was the getting hold of drink. If he went without even for a short time, life turned into hell, battered by dizzy waves. His stomach resonated with pain, as if the lord of the underworld had emerged and were twisting his innards in agonizing torture. As well as physical torture, he underwent mental agony. When he had the strength he wandered around the bookshops, where he saw books from his own hand, distillations of his own spirit, on sale everywhere. People's pleasure in his writing was unabated, and would remain so. His books were reprinted again and again, under different covers, dimensions and prices. He saw people pick them up and buy them, and others come after and buy them too. No-one knew he was the author. But the books brought him no return. He had long since sold off the copyright.

During this time his friends distanced themselves from him. They knew that anyone who met him would have to pay, with either a drink or a handout. Many publishers would no longer receive him, and on his part, he did not dare approach them because he had no manuscripts to show as he had promised in return for fees paid in advance. All he could do was lurch around, dependent on friends and acquaintances who grew fewer by the day. Khru Chuang, his first patron, was really the only one left. No matter how drunk or exhausted, Nori could always find a meal and a bed at Chuang's. Yet Nori did not like going there, because Chuang had changed. He used to be the one urging Nori to drink, but now he exhorted him not to. From the beginning, Chuang had been alarmed by Nori's drinking. His own experience as a drunkard told him that Nori was in danger. When Chuang first saw him take a drink, he understood with the premonition of a regular drinker that if Nori kept it up, he would lose everything, including his life. He said to Nori, "You're different from me. I don't know whether it's a difference in our makeup or what. I take breaks from drinking, so the alcohol only pickles me to preserve me. But when you get going, you don't stop, so the alcohol burns you up. If you don't give it away, you'll soon be dead."

But Chuang's admonition had no effect. Nori dismissed him as a small-time hack writer, not someone prominent in literary circles like himself.

AS things deteriorated, Chuang sent word to Nori's home in Wiset district, and his mother sent his brother to bring him home.

At home, his mother never alluded to his broken promise, or scolded him for it. She tended him as if he were ill with some other disease. She did not refuse him the alcohol that his body craved, but brought it quickly to satiate his longing. Yet she did not overdo it, and after a while the care and attention of his mother and family, combined with the pure country air and nutritious regular diet, led him to recovery. He gradually regained his strength and energy. His mother reduced the alcohol in proportion to the resurgence of his physical strength. Nori was not very old, and his body was able to make a good recovery.

Nori spent a year at home. He regained bodily strength, and his original powers of thought and intellect revived. He no longer drank. But he knew that the country was not the place for him to redeem himself. Once, he had been famous in Bangkok, and had fallen from prominence there through the workings of fate. He would have to redeem himself in Bangkok. When he felt well enough to return to Bangkok, he told his mother. She cried, but did not say anything. He spent days trying to persuade her reasonably that he could not stay on at home when his whole life and fortune were in Bangkok. But every time he raised this she only cried, neither permitting or opposing him. Finally, he tired of waiting for her permission. He disappeared from home one morning without telling anyone.

THE people in the boat that left Ban Phaen that night looked at one of their fellow passengers in puzzlement. He sat alone, with two or three empty bottles beside him. Another was open, ready for more drinking. Passengers going about their honest business did not know who he was, but avoided him when they saw his condition. No-one wanted to go near an old soak. Nori took no notice. His fame and fortune transcended these country folk. His mother and family had tried to keep him drowned in a puddle, but he had struggled out. His mother had attempted to make him give up drinking, and for a while he had. Why did he need to drink in that buffalo hole? Now he was out of the hole, and he struggled to celebrate—to celebrate his imminent return to Bangkok to reclaim his fame and importance. He had ceased to write many years ago, but now he was ready to go again. Words were beginning to struggle inside him like caged birds. Hang on! Hang on! Wait till the proper time and I'll release you to sing and please everyone who listens and hears. Right now I have to drink, to make up for lost time.

Nori lifted his glass and drank. His hand had begun to tremble again. The drink spilled down his front. "What was that?" he thought to himself as he clutched his hand around a small amulet. His mother had asked him to wear it again. He had taken it off once before, and sold the chain for grog, but the amulet was still there. When his brother went to get him from Bangkok he recovered it, and his mother had found another chain for it. Nori laughed quietly to himself as he softly stroked the amulet. What did it matter! Even the amulet was defiled by drink, soaked in drink . . .

The same morning that one of the publishing houses advertised that it was taking orders for the fourth or fifth edition of Nori's latest romantic novel, in a beautiful glossy coloured cover, his body lay on the bank after the rain and storm had abated. People coming and going only noticed a dead man, his hand clasped to his breast. If anyone had bothered to prize open his tightly-clenched fist, they would have found a tiny amulet.

LINCHONG—THE MOTHER

LINCHONG had often pondered in her mind over *karma* and its fruits. But no matter how she scrutinized her past, she could find no possible cause for the great suffering that afflicted her later in life.

Linchong, the only child of a prosperous family, was born at Lat Nam Khem. She was born in the rainy season, when lotus blossoms covered the fields. A few days after her birth, her mother saw the lotuses blooming behind the house where she lay beside her bed of coals, and decided to call her baby daughter Linchong. Linchong grew up to be as beautiful as her name—as pure as a lotus blooming in clear water.

Because she was an only child, her parents lavished all their love on her. She wanted for nothing. At the same time, her mother raised her to be steadfast in virtue. She indicated the results of evil and the pain of vice by pointing out their opposites, and showing the happiness which stemmed from good deeds and the cheer of the heart that is compassionate. Because Linchong's heart was pure and unsullied, the seeds of her mother's teaching blossomed on its fertile soil. She feared *karma* and was repulsed by sin, and put her faith in pure and charitable thought, speech and action.

Her mother's teachings affected her profoundly. She remembered well the time in her childhood when she went playing along the banks of the canal one morning with friends, some of whom carried fishing rods. Later she borrowed one to try her hand, and landed a small fish. The image of the fish struggling before it died was still with her. Afterwards she ran home, as if to escape from the sin she had committed. That night she lay in bed bathed in a cold sweat, fearful of the consequences of having killed a living creature. From then on she was even more afraid of evil, and wished for no further truck with it. She stopped her playmates if she saw them killing living creatures, which made them laugh and tease her, as children are wont to do. But she was neither embarrassed nor offended, and as time went on her reputation for virtue spread.

When she blossomed into adolescence, many young men in the neighbourhood desired Linchong because she was endowed with physical beauty, as well as other qualities. But she was not free with her affections. Her parents were particularly careful about this, as she was their only daughter. Thus, as a young unmarried woman, she spent rather a lot of time at home. In the meantime her parents meticulously selected her life's partner for her, as if searching for a flawless diamond. Eventual-ly, whether because they had known each other in a previous existence or for some other reason, Linchong made up her mind to fall in love with a young man who lived nearby. Even though he was not very well off, her parents did not stand in her way. Nai Sangwian, the man she chose, was diligent and well-mannered. He did not drink or gamble. Linchong ul-timately married Sangwian, and her parents accepted their son-in-law into their home.

Linchong's married life ran smoothly, without obstacles or quarrels. Husband and wife loved each other in harmony, and shared common aims for the future they would build together. They would be solidly established and important in their own social circles, and would raise a good family, praised by all in Lat Nam Khem. What they both wanted most was a child—a child to carry on the family line, to bind the union of their shared life even closer; a child who in childhood would be their delight and in maturity their support. This child would be the hope which proved, at the end of their lives, that life would flourish and multiply, and not end with the death of any one individual.

After marriage, Linchong thought that the charitable acts she had performed ever since she could remember meant she would bear an appealing and beautiful child, who would grow in strength into a good-looking, well-behaved youth. She dreamt of this child—a boy. After that, they could be girls or boys, the more the better. She did not know how many she would have, but their social standing and the productivity of the land, combined with their diligence, set no limits. Both Linchong and her husband felt certain that no matter how many children they had, they would easily be able to care for them.

But it seems to be a law of nature—or nature's cruelty where the human race is concerned—that the more fervently something is desired and sought after, the more seemingly distant and difficult of attainment it becomes. Linchong was better off than most. Her parents had provided material possessions, so that they wanted for nothing. They were well-equipped to earn their living, and had never had any worries in that direction. As for the qualities of the heart, they had accumulated enough merit to feel satisfied with their situation. They endured no struggle or hardship, and found contentment in their surroundings—the bright green of the fields, the murmuring of the bamboo in the wind, the warm, sweet smell of the buffalo and cattle in their pen, the sound of fish surfacing under the house in the wet season. But these were not enough to repress certain desires—in particular the desire for a child, of which there was no sign, even after long years of marriage.

At times Linchong lay in bed with her husband listening to the rain falling on the roof, the raindrops splashing on the surface of the water in the watercourse in front of the house, and the wind blowing the drenching rain over the fields. She knew that rain was nature's lifeblood. When it fell on dry ground, sleeping seeds would awaken and expand in the dampness of the rain to put down roots in the earth to imbibe sustenance for growth and life. At those moments she felt new life all around her. Every grain of rice sown was pushing up shoots of a paler green than an artist could ever capture. The sound of fish popping up softly from the water reminded her that the mother serpent-head fish lived under the house, looking after its school of offspring. When she washed the dishes at the foot of the landing she saw hundreds of tiny, red, baby serpent-heads, like little flames, bobbing up and down and swimming under the steps while the mother fish hid behind a post, watching with close attention. At that time of night Linchong could only lie awake, sighing with sorrow, thinking of burgeoning life around her, great and small, existing and about to come into existence. But it seemed there was a dryness within her—a lack of fertility, a lack of some starting point from which a life might grow. No matter how much the rain fell, nor how much the rain-soaked land nourished plant and animal life, Linchong saw herself as barren, still without hope of the child her heart desired. She lay tossing restlessly. Her throat felt parched, but she dared not turn over for fear of disturbing the husband who lay beside her.

FIVE years of marriage passed without a child. Husband and wife looked despairingly at each other. Their life together was happy enough, but without the child they both wanted, it seemed empty and meaningless. During this time Linchong and her husband had jointly performed acts of merit more frequently than usual, and more than others in the neighbourhood. Whenever there was a collection for a new temple or prayer hall or monastery, or for giving new robes to the monks, Linchong quickly handed over some money as her share. As she did so she always prayed for the fulfilment of her wish for a child. She rose early every day to cook rice for the monks, and waited at the head of the stairs until all the monks paddling by on their daily begging round had left the waterways. Whenever there was a major sermon at the temple, Linchong and Sangwian only attended to the part dealing with birth. All the time she was preparing the offerings for the monks she prayed, with body and soul, and with every finger engaged in the intricate arrangements, for a child. She only asked for one child, boy or girl, no matter how ugly. All she wanted was a child of her womb, to love and cherish and delight in, like everyone else who had children so easily without any prayers or acts of merit at all.

During that period, Linchong got her husband to accompany her to any Buddha image reputed to have sacred powers, or any shrine with a spirit possessing the supernatural force to bestow children on petitioners, to plead for a child. The couple braved the way, no matter how far, without thought for hardship or expense.

Whether because of these meritorious acts, the supernatural powers of the sacred objects she had appealed to, or her own acts in a previous existence, Linchong fell pregnant at the beginning of her sixth year of marriage.

WHEN she knew for certain, Linchong felt light with overflowing happiness. She drifted into beautiful reveries. Her life was full. Everything seemed to have meaning, direction and order, and was not merely a result of arbitrary fate, as she had thought previously. Her husband Sangwian was pleased, and anxiously supported her. He took on any tasks he considered too heavy for her. When he looked at the pregnant belly, now showing clearly, he smiled to himself and sighed with fulfilled happiness. When Linchong woke at night she was no longer restless or lonely. She lay smiling to herself in the darkness. The sounds of wind and rain, and the little noises of the animals in the fields and waterways, turned into lullabies, signals of life, interconnected with the life developing inside her. She felt the baby in her womb wriggle, and turn gently. Sometimes her flesh crept with happiness and excitement at the miracle of life. But at other times, she felt a love more forceful than any other, squeeze her heart until she could barely stand it. Love, affection, and compassion for the tiny life that was a part of her own, yet separate, welled up inside her and spilled over in warm tears, pouring down her cheeks.

Linchong took care with her pregnancy, and her stomach grew. In that time she prepared the things she would need for the birth, insofar as custom allowed. Sangwian went out in his boat to chop every block of wood himself and stacked them neatly on the verandah at the back of the house for his wife's lying-in fire. Each block was the same size, lovingly chopped and chosen. Relatives, and all who knew of the couple's hopes and desires, were happy when they heard that Linchong was to have a child. They gave her their blessing, and waited in excitement for the day to come.

One evening, in the drizzling rain, Sangwian moored the boat in front of the landing and said to his wife, "Linchong,

I'm going to do a bit of fishing. The fish should bite well in this rain. If anything happens, send someone for me at the bend in the waterway. I might go into the fields a way, but I shouldn't be long. If they're biting well, I'll be back late."

"Don't go, it's sinful," Linchong called back from the house. But Sangwian laughed, and paddled off. This was not the first time she had invoked merit and sin to stop him doing something. She often did, and he listened good humouredly. Anyway, vegetables and fish were vegetables and fish, and still brought in a handy income. It was better than sitting idle.

Linchong awoke late at night. She encountered an empty space on the mattress when she stretched her arm out beside her, and so knew that her husband had not returned yet. After that she slept fitfully, listening for the sound of the oars hitting the water, the chain mooring the boat to the head of the steps, the creaking of the stairs, and the footsteps on the verandah, the signs that her husband had returned. By dawn, those sounds were still unheard. Linchong got up and washed. Then she went into the kitchen to prepare the cooking in readiness for her husband, who would be back soon, with a boat full of fish.

Time passed until late morning. The sun was up and burning, and the boards on the verandah, wet from the previous night's rain, had been dried out by the sun's rays. Three or four young men rowed a boat up and moored it at the head of the steps, then jointly carried the sopping, lifeless body of Nai Sangwian up the stairs. They crossed the outer landing to lay it out on the floor underneath the eaves at the front of the house. Water dripped off the body onto the landing, leaving a trail as if someone had dragged a wet cloth over the floor.

"Wian had a cramp, Chong," one of the young men said to Linchong, who watched the scene as if in a dream. "He got a cramp in the water . . . he must have been down groping for bait at night. But he was out on his own. Who could've got to him in time? We were rowing past in the morning, and saw the empty boat moored there, so we stopped to see . . . so we could only bring . . . that." The young man pointed to the body, and said brokenly, "We could only bring him home."

Linchong sat absolutely still, her eyes fixed on what, yesterday, had been her husband. He had been alive, breathing, laughing, with a warm body . . . and now, this sodden thing, his features so pale as to be barely recognizable, hands clenched, showing that he had struggled before he died . . . A soft sound like a hiccup emanated from her throat, and she fainted.

WHEN she recovered, she knew at once that her time had come. The pain she felt then was unlike anything she had ever experienced. Fortunately for Linchong, the pain caused by life clamouring to be brought into the world came at the same time as her emotional pain over life extinguished from the world. The physical pain, which felt as though someone had pulled apart all the bones below her waist at the back, dulled some of the emotional pain and sorrow. When her relatives were certain of her condition, they helped lift her inside. Other relatives stayed with Sangwian's body in the traditional manner. Birth and death attacked Linchong's house together. Neither could be halted—events had to be left to take their course. People could only cover up, for both birth and death, so they would not offend the eye.

Linchong had a son, perfectly formed. He cried lustily at birth, a sign that he would grow into a strong, solid child. She tried to stop herself from thinking of her dead husband, and refused to shed tears of sorrow for fear that her milk would sour and poison the child. As she lay by the birth-fire, she gazed on the face of the child asleep in the bamboo cradle, seeking support from the new life in place of that which had been so hastily and unexpectedly extinguished. At times she could barely restrain her thoughts, because she knew that each piece of smouldering wood had been gathered by her husband's labours, and was being devoured by flames just like his body, which the relatives had taken and cremated until nothing was left but ashes.

Once free from the lying-in, Linchong set herself to bringing up the baby. For solace, she held fast to the merit she had created. Even though her husband's death had been fate of a kind, having the child was sheer good fortune. Her charity and generosity, her vows and pledges, had not been in vain. She shut her eyes and refused to listen to her instincts, and would not accept that the baby, whom she called Daeng, was ill-fated. Instead, she saw him as the reward of merit, coming to her aid in times of suffering. Had Daeng not been born then, and had she lost her husband first, it was anybody's guess as to how her life would have been. For this reason, Daeng became the centre of Linchong's life, a precious possession, hard won and irreplaceable. She poured out all the love that was in her onto him. And that love was far in excess of the ordinary mother-love, because not only did circumstances make her love her child more than was normal, but all the love her parents had lavished on her was passed on to the baby a thousandfold.

Daeng was an easy baby. Not delicate or sickly, he grew by the day. He rolled over at the right time, pushed and crawled when the time came, and also learned to stand and started toddling like other children. But Linchong began to notice that her beloved child was different when it came time for him to talk. Daeng could not speak as other children did. Everyone expressed their surprise, but in response to the sympathetic remarks of well-meaning friends and relations Linchong could only say, "Daeng's probably a bit tongue-tied. Most likely it won't matter. He'll start talking when he's ready, and then he'll be a real chatterbox."

Linchong tried not to think about his slowness. Instead she dismissed it from her mind, and continued to nurture him lovingly. She took no notice of people's remarks and questions.

Thus when Daeng began to talk recognizably, when he was about three, Linchong was exceptionally pleased and happy. He started to learn the various forms of 'yes', as a younger child would, and could eventually say 'mother'. She nearly floated with joy the first time he said it, and wept freely. From his birth she had known she was a 'mother', but her feeling had been one-sided. It was complete when Daeng, her most important bond, said that she was his mother—that word which referred to half the human world, half the earth, half the galaxy. The depth of its significance was indescribable. Used in certain contexts, the word could make people refrain from evil and do good, and in other contexts, drive them mad enough to kill in rage. The one word, with two syllables . . . 'mother'.

But Daeng's speech did not progress as Linchong had expected. He could only say simple words to indicate physical needs—eating and sleeping, asking for rice, or water, or sweets. It was not until he was about five years old that it first struck her that he was different. Superficially, he was strong and healthy like other children his age, or even stronger.

That day Daeng had been up to more mischief than usual, so Linchong scolded him. But as she spoke, the look he gave her made her start, and lower her voice immediately. In that look she had glimpsed the incomprehension of an infant, too young to know right from wrong, or the desires and good intentions of others. The terror she had seen in his eyes did not stem from guilt and the fear of being caught, because he was unable to tell whether he was doing right or wrong. It was the terror of a baby's instinctive response to being startled by a loud noise. When Daeng heard Linchong speak crossly, he was frightened, and rushed to hold her tightly with a baby's confidence that his mother would protect him from danger.

She sat holding him for some time, until he had calmed down and slipped off to play again. Linchong felt fearful as she sat watching him, now convinced that her child was not like others. Although physically developed, he was still a baby. She watched his manner, and the way he played like a younger child —a child of two or three rather than a five year-old. He shook or banged everything he got hold of to make a noise. She watched the way he laughed randomly, like a baby. The more she saw, the clearer it became, and the more disheartened she felt. She could not say that her son showed any signs of physical illness or disease, so she did not know how to set about curing him. Depression overcame her.

Fortunately for Linchong, the truth had quite escaped her. She did not know, because she had never bothered to find out, that body and mind do not develop at the same rate in everyone. In some cases the mind develops to a certain stage, then stops completely, leaving the body to its physical pro-gression. Linchong did not know that there was nothing physically wrong with Daeng. He would progress normally through childhood to adolescence, and decline into old age, like any human being. But for whatever reason or quirk of fate, his mental development had been arrested at two or three years old, and would never develop further. For the rest of his life, until the day he died, Daeng would have a mental age of three, no matter what his physical age. If Linchong had known this, she would also have understood that her hope of seeing Daeng as an adult, her support in old age, was not to be fulfilled. Because his mental development had ceased in infancy, Daeng would rely entirely on Linchong for support. She would have the burden of an infant until she breathed her last. Fate had dealt her a heavy blow. She drew small consolation from the know-ledge that Daeng would always love her deeply, with the undiminishing love of an infant.

But because she did not know the whole truth, only that there were certain things which were not right with her child at the time, she hoped that one day there would be a way of bringing him back to normality. And as long as she held this hope, Linchong was not unduly troubled.

When Daeng was little, no-one noticed that he was different from other children. Children, whether three or five, are just children to most adults. But Daeng grew up, unstoppable. As days, months, and years passed, so his age rose correspond-ingly. By the time he was nine or ten the difference was quite obvious. Daeng ate, slept, spoke and performed his toilet like a three year-old. Regardless of what Linchong taught him, he stared at her with an infant's incomprehension. She sighed whenever she encountered this direct gaze, and would sometimes pull him to her and cry with pity and affection.

The difference was particularly marked when he was with children his own age, or younger, because they all knew what proper behaviour was. He tagged on to the group in all inno-cence. He ran and watched whatever games they were playing, without understanding. If other children teased or bullied him, he burst into tears like a three year-old. At times smaller, younger, children shouted and threatened him, and he cried and ran away in fright. Daeng became a plaything for the children round about to tease and bully, the way they liked to bully and mercilessly poke fun at animals.

EVENTUALLY Linchong had to keep him inside and not allow him out to play with the other children. But it was too late. They knew that Daeng was different, that he was crazy or a mute and was fun to tease. Even when Daeng's mother did not let him out of the house, the children gathered on the landing next door and taunted him gleefully. From time to time they threw sticks or stones to startle him. If he went to chase them away, they ran off, and returned later. Daeng lived in fear, and ran to hold on to his mother and rest his head on her, like a tormented and terrified infant. Then she tried to kiss and comfort him. She bit her lip and cried despairingly, burdened by the massive weight of anxiety.

After the children had noticed Daeng's peculiarity, the adults in the neighbourhood began to gossip and spread the rumour that Linchong's child was a crazy mute. Her relatives regarded her anxiously. Some came to visit, and even though they did not discuss Daeng, she knew that they had come to look at him and see whether he was as different as they had heard. No matter what excuses she made for him, their case rested on the sight of Daeng ambling aimlessly around the place. He was proof to all that the rumours were absolutely correct.

And, as was natural in a small, closely-knit group, the majority began to distance themselves from anyone unusual or somehow different from ordinary people, as if to weed that person out of society and eject them from the group. The neighbourhood began to behave this way toward Linchong. They saw her as alien, separate, differentiated from the group. When she took Daeng anywhere with her everyone stared, and whispered when she had passed from sight. She knew perfectly well that they were talking about their pity and sympathy for her. But she knew even better that what they called pity was merely human nature manifesting its pleasure in the suffering and misfortunes of others. Her misfortune was particularly apparent, because she had always been so fortunate. Born with physical and material endowments, she was conspicuously pious. Her troubles, it could be clearly seen, attracted the malicious pleasure and interest of those people who felt that they had been less fortunate than Linchong in the past.

Linchong could no longer hide the truth from herself. Daeng was now approaching adolescence, but his mental level was unchanged. With every day of physical maturity, his emotional immaturity and pitifully arrested mental development became starker. Anyone who saw him knew at once, without being told, that he was different. Linchong had to admit it too. She could not imagine what *karma* could have caused it. The more she thought about it, the more she was driven nearly demented with despair. She spent whole nights reviewing her life to see which of her actions could have produced such a result. But she could not think of any. She became increasingly depressed. In the end all she could do was to get up and light the lamp, and sit hugging her knees looking at Daeng, who slept with the innocence of a baby. She could only weep.

Once she had accepted that her child was different, Linchong also admitted that she could not simply leave Daeng to see out his destiny. She had hoped against hope that one day he would miraculously recover, but her hope went unfulfilled. She could not put it off, or wait any longer. From then on, she brought any good doctor she heard of to treat her child, whether a medical doctor, a doctor of spells or a doctor of unguents. But the result was always the same. Each doctor treated Daeng for a time, then disappeared, after Linchong had paid unstintingly for the cost of treatment. Daeng was left in his original condition, with no sign of improvement. When she realized that a doctor had left, she hugged her son and cried, then gritted her teeth and set to work with a future devoid of all hope.

LINCHONG'S situation worsened. The expense of numerous doctors and medicines, coupled with the sorrow and bitterness, gave her little spirit to set herself to earning a living. Poor, with a helpless, dependent child to support, she looked fearfully to the future. Linchong thought ahead to her own death, and to Daeng's. The world seemed a very bleak place.

But where there was life there was hope. When Linchong heard of a learned and holy monk in Nonthaburi province, who cured the sick with incantations and holy water, she wasted no time. Quickly, she packed a few necessities and took Daeng by boat to Sena district, to catch the night passenger ferry to Nonthaburi.

Sitting by Daeng in the boat, amidst the sounds of wind and rain, Linchong felt a lightness and relief she had not known for a long time. Because as they waited for the boat at Ban Phaen, Daeng had shown signs of being like other children. She did not know whether this was because Ban Phaen had been full of strangers, unacquainted with Daeng's background, who had not had any reason to stare. Nonetheless, Linchong allowed herself to think that Daeng was improving, and feeling this way, she had faith in the miracle to be wrought by the abbot at Nonthaburi. She was certain that this time he would be cured. She would return home with a son who was just like other people's children, his mother's pride and joy.

If Linchong alone had jumped into the water when the boat tilted before capsizing, she could probably have struggled out of its way and survived. But the unselfishness of a mother's love surpasses even life itself. Linchong turned to tug at Daeng's arm to get him to leave with her. Instead he clung to the rails, and refused to let go. With the instinctive terror of a baby, he held fast to whatever was closest—the boat rails. Linchong tried to pull him away with all the force she could muster, calling his name at the top of her voice. Daeng let go, crying out the single word 'mother', and threw himself into her arms. He clung tightly around her neck with all the force of a child approaching manhood. They both sank.

Next morning, the villagers at the scene of the ferry accident had to turn away from the pitiful sight. On the riverbank in the soft early morning sun mother and child lay dead, locked in an embrace. Some muttered softly to themselves, "Mother and child dying together in an embrace . . . how tragic! What *karma* could have brought them to this end? . . ."

CHAN—THE SOLDIER

CHAN was born in a house in the fields on the outskirts of Phak Hai district. His parents were farmers, with a holding of about forty *rai*. Twelve *rai* were behind the house. The rest was further away, and was rented out to cover the cost of an equivalent area of farmland closer to home. Chan was one of three. He was the eldest son. His next brother was named Pan, because of a red birthmark (*pan*) on his shoulder, and his younger sister's name was Won.

Chan's childhood and youth were like those of other children in the neighbourhood. As soon as he could run well, he helped his parents tend the buffaloes, and when he was a little older he went fishing and looking for edible plants to eat. He helped plough and sow in the rice-planting season, and assisted with harvesting and winnowing the rice at harvest time. He never felt different from his friends; that is, he did not think he was any worse, or in any way inferior. Everyone in the neighbourhood was of equal standing. Small differences in wealth did not alter their position as neighbours or set them apart. At the very least, the vegetation around the edges of the fields and the fish in the waterways belonged equally to all, and whoever had the wit to get them would not go hungry. When Chan was a boy, food and other items were not too expensive, so everyone could live comfortably, rich or poor.

As a child, Chan was taught in the same way as the other neighbourhood children. If parents had the time, they taught their children to know right from wrong and good from bad, as the situation arose, according to the moral precepts handed down from olden times, without questioning the rationale for them. The explanations handed down by their parents and grandparents seemed sufficient, and no-one thought to waste time picking and choosing and raising objections. The teach-ings Chan received were more like prohibitions—not to speak falsehoods, not to covet the wives and daughters of others, not to cheat or steal, and not to behave like a hooligan. As for certain of the precepts, such as those which forbade the killing of living creatures or the drinking of intoxicating liquor, his father spoke of these, if he mentioned them at all, in an undertone without conviction because he went fishing every day and drank expansively with his friends when in high spirits.

When Chan was free from work around the house, he was sent off to study with the old abbot at the temple, with a number of other pupils. Through the familiarity of rote learning, he eventually learned to read and write.

Life took a serious turn the year he was conscripted, or, as they said in the neighbourhood, sent off to the soldiery. Chan's parents, especially his mother, seemed very agitated before the selection for military service. Whenever she heard word of any master of magical rites or any holy water that could help save men from military service, she took Chan to take part in the rites or be anointed with the lustral water. She also made pledges to the household deities and the spirits of various shrines to protect him. She planned that he would become a monk if he escaped conscription this time. Then she would be able to get to heaven on the tail of her eldest son's saffron robe.

But when the day eventually came for officials to measure the young men's chests at the district office, Chan's measurement and medical clearance were first class. They made him sit to one side on his own and refused to let him go home. At noon his mother brought him a parcel of food, and looked at him red-eyed, on the verge of tears. On the one hand he felt sorry for her, and did not want her to suffer, but another part of him wanted to be a soldier. The soldiers' uniforms that he saw men wearing looked smart and strong, and made him want to wear one. People who had been in the army had told him about the fun and glamour of Bangkok. Not to be outdone, Chan felt he would like to see it too. That afternoon he drew the con-script's red ballot. He heard his mother burst into tears outside, but deep down he was not really perturbed.

Liam was another from his home district conscripted in that round. They had been mates since childhood, and were close friends in adolescence as well. Liam enjoyed a good time. He did not have many worries and did not take too much notice of anything. Whatever happened, he could always lift the spirits of those around him by bursting into song. With Liam as a fellow conscript sitting beside him, and all the other new recruits, in the boat bound for the divisional headquarters in Bangkok, Chan felt nothing out of the ordinary. He was unafraid, because he had a close friend with him and was beginning to realize that the army could be fun.

"We're lucky, Chan," said Liam, sitting in the boat.

"Why's that, Liam?" asked Chan.

"Now we've got the chance to see Bangkok," he said contentedly. "They say it's great fun. I don't know when we would've had the chance if we hadn't got in in this round."

"But they say being a soldier is a tough business," Chan said uncertainly.

"How hard is hard?" Liam said. "People like us suffer hardship anywhere. In the planting season, we have to plough and transplant. In the rainy season, we take the buffalo to its pen and become its slave, eternally going out in the boat to get grass for it to eat its never-ending fill. I'm game for any drill or anything they give you to do in the army—it couldn't be heavier than the work at home. Uncle Plian once told me they only drill at set times, you're okay after that. And no matter how difficult, it's only for two years. Blink and it'll be over. Then I'm not going to mess around with anybody, I'm going to find myself a fantastic wife, just you wait and see.

"I might be a soldier,
But at least I'm not a... "

The end of the jingle made Chan and all the other passengers laugh. Chan did not know where he got them from, but Liam had an appropriate folk opera jingle for every occasion.

Chan stayed at the barracks for two or three days. Before prayers one night, an old sergeant came to instruct the company. He spoke clearly and distinctly, pointing out movingly to the new recruits the advantages of being a soldier.

"Everyone should know how beneficial this opportunity to become a soldier is," he began. He went on to speak of a man's duty to his country, faith and king, and other interesting matters. At one point he said, "Let's consider it. As soldiers, you're given all manner of things. They provide uniforms, hat to boots. Who's going to give you these back home? I never even wore shoes till I joined the army. Shirts, trousers—you get the lot—right down to mattresses and mosquito nets, so you don't have to worry. On top of that, every month you're paid spending money. Now where else are you going to find this? If you can't read or write, they'll teach you. People instruct you in all kinds of subjects. Regular meals, regular sleep, and you get one full day's rest every seven days. Do you get this back home? When your parents need you for work, you're there every day, in the burning sun, no weekends. They complain when you want to go out for a good time. Here, someone blows a trumpet when it's time to sleep, and there's another trumpet blast when it's time to wake up. At meal times they summon you by trumpet. Who makes sure you eat and sleep at home? Who'd wait for us if we didn't make it at mealtime? They look after you far better than at home. You should realize that it's your good fortune to have joined the army. It's a great boon to be a soldier. You should all be pleased and proud."

Chan thought about what the sergeant was saying, and agreed with him. But Liam, sitting beside him, laughed quietly to himself with great amusement. Chan could not see what he was laughing about.

From then on, Chan took an interest in the business of soldiering. He heeded the instruction, the discipline, and the orders of the commanding officer. His initial feeling that being a soldier was to be a two-year endurance trial changed. The training, drills and discipline became part of his life; an important part, better and more secure than when he had been entirely free. Liam observed him, and said, "Chan! If you take it all so seriously you're sure to make it to lieutenant one day!"

In fact, at that time nothing was further from Chan's thoughts than being a commissioned officer, but he just laughed and did not respond. His interest in his duties and activities did not let up, so it was inevitable that he became a first-class private in his second year. As the time for his discharge approached, the troop commander called him in and said, "I see that you've performed your duty well, Chan. You're one of the best soldiers I've come across."

Chan, standing to attention in front of the company captain's desk, nearly floated with joy. After all, what makes people happier than recognition of their merit? The company captain went on in a more informal tone, "Chan, what do you intend to do after you're discharged?"

Chan stood even straighter, as was proper when addressing a commanding officer, and said "I . . . I'm going back home to help my parents with farming, sir."

"Are you the only child?"

"No, sir. My parents have two other children."

The company captain rapped his fingers on the table for a moment, as if thinking something over, then said, "Chan, I wouldn't say this if you were an only child. But you've got family to help out at home. I think you should re-enlist after your discharge. If you keep going at this rate, it won't be long before you gain entry to the non-commissioned officer's training course, the technical course, and after that, you'll probably get the chance to become a commissioned officer with due rank and substance. Think it over carefully. Don't hurry, there's still time. But let me know what you decide. I'll support you all the way. I've considered what I'm saying, and I wouldn't have said it if I didn't think you had real potential."

The company captain began to leaf through the papers on his desk, a signal for Chan to click his heels loudly, about turn, and leave the room. But he did not do so. He straightened up, fixed his gaze on the company captain's three gold stars and his polished, gleaming sash, and unable to suppress his feeling, burst out, "Captain . . . Captain sir, I . . . want to re-enlist. I'm not leaving."

The company captain looked up at him for a long time, then asked, "Have you thought this over carefully, Chan?"

"I have, sir," he responded, brusquely and clearly as soldiers do. At that moment he felt so close to the company captain that it was almost as if they were related. They were professional soldiers, real soldiers, together.

The company captain walked over and slapped him on the back, saying, "Stand at ease, Chan, not at attention. There's only the two of us. Smoke?"

He held out the packet, and when Chan took a cigarette, lit it from the one in his hand. He said, "I thought you'd agree. Terrific! Thanks for that. I'll arrange everything, don't you worry. Let me know if anything crops up. I'll be glad to help if you've got any worries."

Chan did not tell anyone of his agreement with the company captain, until one day Liam said, "Chan! We'll be going home in a few days. We've served out our sentence!"

Liam was open-mouthed in amazement when Chan told him he intended to remain a soldier. He looked as though he was about to advise him to change his mind, but stayed silent because he could not think how to put it. The day his batch was discharged, Chan saw his friends off and watched them leave with regret, especially in the case of Liam, who was from the same village. That was probably the only time Chan wondered whether he had made the wrong decision. The sheer delight of all the young men at the prospect of returning home dismayed him, because he could not share in it. The feeling lingered while all was quiet and uneventful, but subsided when the new batch of conscripts arrived. It was replaced by a sense of responsibility. Chan, or First-Class Private Chan, had entered government service as a professional soldier ready to make as brilliant a career as his physical and mental strength and perseverance would allow.

Having taken up a profession for life, and sacrificed another kind of life for that profession, it was natural that the life Chan had taken securely in his grasp would proceed to carry him a long way along his desired route. Within eight or nine years, after a period which seemed to be full of study and instruction, he returned once more to his original company.

His return was very different from his arrival. He had come as a young country boy who had just been conscripted, and was tasting life away from home for the first time. Everything seemed strange and wondrous. He had to be told why things happened the way they did, and what purpose they served. Chan the raw young recruit knew nothing about anything, even himself. But the Chan who came back was not the old Chan. He returned as a commissioned officer, a platoon commander, with a name more befitting a commissioned officer—Second Lieutenant Surawut.

His new life and status were full of pomp, of people who held him in awe and respect. Soldiers saluted wherever he went. His fellow officers, largely from families of the well-born, wealthy businessmen, nobles who had served the crown for generations, or even the royal family itself, accepted Surawut and never asked him about his birth or background. Should any of his fellow soldiers ask, he was ready to say that he was a farmer's son, born in the country, who had joined the army as a conscript. But as no-one asked, he saw no need to tell them.

For the next ten years, Chan the country bumpkin from Phak Hai was swallowed up more and more by commissioned officer Surawut, and eventually disappeared altogether. At first Surawut kept in touch with home in a desultory way. He learned that his parents were delighted that their eldest son was an important personage. They did not dare visit him, however.

Old and frail, they feared he would suffer because they did not know how to conduct themselves. They wanted him to come home to be admired. Surawut kept putting off his home-coming, caught up in official duties or other business. But the real reason was that Surawut, now a captain, had no desire to resurrect the spirit of Chan the country bumpkin within the outward form of the honoured soldier, universally respected, who mixed in high society with gentlefolk whose thought, speech and lifestyle were of a different order from those of the people Chan had grown up with.

After his parents' death, his brother Pan came to see him to discuss property and inheritance. This amounted to some cash, a little gold, and over forty *rai* that had been their sustenance. Pan was a true farmer. His complexion, looks, manner and speech gave his country origins away. Pan knew this better than anyone, and did not aspire to equality with his exalted brother. He sat on the floor to talk to his brother, who was seated on a chair. When Surawut had agreed to hand over all his parents' property, now without meaning or value to him, to Pan and his sister Won, with a written declaration as evidence, Pan excused himself and asked the officer's aide for a meal behind the kitchen. That night he was given a bed out the back with the aide, and next morning he took his leave.

From that day, the bonds between Surawut and his family were severed and his antecedents were lost in the past. He married a woman of good family, in a public ceremony. Many senior officials came to bless the union. Surawut lived his chosen life confidently. It was full of honour and prestige: the honour of his wife's family; the honour of his army rank; the honour of the respect and obedience of those in his command; the honour of ruling a large number of people with firm discipline. His every order was absolute. No-one doubted, questioned, or disagreed. Surawut's world was filled with honour and discipline, honour which could make the nerves tauten and the blood pump as effectively as expensive liquor. Others in Surawat's position, who were steadier and more self-confident than he, might have been able to exert more self-control and avoid intoxication. But what can one do when nature has made some strong, others weak; some firm, others not? What could be done when Surawut lacked inner strength, lacked an enduring foundation to support him in times of turmoil or shock? Given his character, it was inevitable that Surawut would become intoxicated by his high standing, regarding external accoutrements and trappings as the real core of life.

The eleven years following his marriage passed so quickly that Surawut was unable to prepare himself for what lay ahead. But one day he sat down and went over his accounts at home. What would he have after he received his discharge order and became a service pensioner? He would have a plaintive invalid wife who needed constant treatment, a nine-year-old son who had to be educated, a pension which he thought would be adequate to live on, and the honour of a lieutenant-colonel which he would have to preserve to his dying day. That was all. Yet he knew that his rank would have to be the pillar around which the rest of his life revolved. His future conduct would depend upon that pillar, as would that of his wife and son. His standard of living and his lifestyle would all revolve around it, because honour was all he would have left.

Even though Surawut did not feel particularly disheartened just then, the situation in his country at the time, when it was neither one party or the other, depressed him more by the day. The price of food and other items no longer remained cheap and stable as they once had. The very war in which he had played a major part as the commander of a battalion, made everything more and more expensive, and the only things that were falling in value were money, human life, and honour. But Lieutenant-Colonel Surawut still put a high value on honour. When his pension dwindled, insufficient to support the whole family honourably at the standard he had set for them, he had to look around for work. Work which, according to his own requirements, had to be in keeping with the dignity and position of a soldier of no mean rank.

Lieutenant-Colonel Surawut journeyed about looking for work in various places for a long time. In any one day, he would first go here and then there looking for work from all his friends and acquaintances. He said he was not particular, and all his friends interpreted this as not particular, whether it was for the government or for state enterprises or for private firms. There was no problem about the position he would fill. How could someone who had been a lieutenant-colonel work as a coolie, lifting and carrying, or as an office clerk or junior official? Work appropriate to his honour and to his former status and position would have to be at senior management level, at the seat of power commanding others, with responsibility and firm discipline, in keeping with the responsible post he had occupied previously.

As time went on, Surawut began to understand that jobs suited to his position and honour were not easy to find, because everybody wanted them. They were always reserved especially for family and cronies. When he first met his old friends, they greeted him warmly and offered him a seat, cigarettes, hot and cold drinks. They asked after his welfare, and assured him that they were happy to help, and were always at his service. But when the discharged lieutenant-colonel mentioned his intention of looking for work, their attitudes changed. Some avoided his gaze and said awkwardly that the business was still too small and undeveloped; some were evasive and avoided any commitment, which meant that if he went to see them again they would be busy and unable to see him; closer friends told him frankly that there was only clerical or coolie work, which was his if he wanted it. Lieutenant-Colonel Surawut would sigh and set off again. The increasing impoverishment of his lifestyle, and the constant barrage of disappointment, made him act even more imposingly as befitted an officer. Instead of bowing his head or walking hunched over, hopelessly, he stood taller and straighter—shoulders back, chin up. Had anyone observed him closely, they would have seen that the eyes which had known the authority of command were losing their sparkle and brightness.

IF Lieutenant-Colonel Surawut had been a civilian in government service at the same salary level as a lieutenant-colonel, and had not commanded a battalion or been a provincial army commander; if his wife had worked for a living and not been enervated in body and spirit by her genteel birth—the two of them might have been able to help each other prop up their lives to suit their new position, and to bring up their child adequately. But as neither of them were like that, they had no way of avoiding the hardships that befell the family. Their son had to leave school, and his wife eventually died from lack of medicines and the will to battle against poverty, leaving him bereft.

After he had put together all the money he had left, and raised more by selling a number of antiques, Lieutenant-Colonel Surawut arranged his wife's cremation in a final gesture of honour. He gave up the little wooden house that they had been renting at an exorbitant rate since his retirement, and took his son by boat back to his old home in Phak Hai. All their possessions were packed loosely into a single suitcase.

He returned in the hope that he could live freely, having some authority over the villagers. As no other job offered him a suitable position, he would go into agriculture in a big way. He would be the head of the whole neighbourhood. True, the people in his old village were country folk, and he might have to instruct them a bit, but what did it matter, he had instructed reams of country folk in the past. Countless batches of rural recruits had been under his command. He thought of the proverb 'Better a leader in hell than a disciple in heaven'. Bangkok had rejected him, so he would live in the country. He would prove to the world that he was born to lead, that he was a man of honour whom everyone respected, no matter where he fell. He disembarked from the ferry at Phak Hai district, and with what amounted to almost all of the money he had left, he hired a motor boat for the two of them to sail majestically along the waterway to the steps of the house.

His family were delighted to see them. His brother Pan was well-off. Won had married and left home. Both had masses of children, girls and boys, some of whom were approaching adolescence. They all clustered happily around their relatives, newly returned after a long absence. Everyone genuinely welcomed them, and assured them wholeheartedly that they could stay as long as they liked. They told him to make use of their homes and property as he pleased. What did not please Chan, and made him most uncomfortable, was that Lieutenant-Colonel Surawut disappeared the moment he clapped eyes on his family. The decorated army officer, rank lieutenant-colonel, with a history of meritorious service, vanished. Only 'Chan' or 'Uncle Chan' resounded through the house.

"See here, Chan! This is Prung, my eldest. Prung! Come and

say hello to Uncle Chan!"

"This is my Waew. She was so sickly as a baby I thought we'd never bring her through. Waew! Don't you know Uncle Chan? Watch it or I'll . . . "

That was it . . . gone were his honourable career and the life he had forged through his diligence and self-sacrifice. He had left home as Chan, and by his return home had reverted to that identity. Nothing had changed. Everybody was visibly delighted. Sincerely, they assured him of their support. What was the point, though, when everyone saw him as 'Chan' or 'Uncle Chan', who had eventually returned home after a long absence to be looked after and kept happy by his younger brother and sister and nieces and nephews. But Chan had not given up hope. Maybe somebody in the neighbourhood would know, would understand his rank and position sufficiently to explain to others that he was a not an ordinary villager, but a man of honour. The headman, in constant touch with the government, would be the one to know him in his rightful position, and would know the correct procedures for communicating with distinguished persons. He wanted the neighbourhood to under-stand his identity and position correctly from the outset. Otherwise, he would not be able to proceed successfully with his plan to be a leader and commander of the people. He had a vision of a vast field, all the farmers labouring earnestly in an orderly manner, following the orders he had issued.

That evening, after a meal where his relatives sat in a circle and ate with their hands, and he managed clumsily because he was accustomed to a now unavailable spoon and fork, Surawut boarded the small boat for Pan's son to take him to the headman's. It was twilight, and torches and fires were being lit. He looked around at the countryside he had left so long ago. He could only recognize bits and pieces, because nearly everything had changed.

The boat moored at the bottom of the steps in front of a large wooden house. It was solid, as befitted the house of the village headman. Surawut went up the stairs and walked straight in, his nephew at his heels. A kerosene lamp blazed brightly under the awning at the front of the house. An elderly man, plump and bald, sat cross-legged in a sarong, shirtless. He had a glass and a bottle of spirits at his side, and numerous bowls of food in front of him. Surawut was sure he must be the headman, so he walked directly through to him. When he was standing close, the headman looked up, his hand over his eyes to shade the glare, glanced over, and asked, "Who is it? Who's there?"

"My name is Lieutenant-Colonel Surawut," he said simply. "I've just arrived here, so I came to make your acquaintance."

According to the plan he had envisaged, the headman would get up and hurriedly pay his respects, then invite him to be seated somewhere appropriate to his honourable position. He would rush inside to put a shirt on neatly, and come out and speak politely. But no . . . not at all . . . The headman peered at him again, then opened his mouth and roared with laughter, showing his mottled and gappy teeth, and said, "Hell! Chan, you old bastard! I thought it was somebody important! Where have you been all these years? I thought you must've been dead!"

"I . . . I . . . Ah," Surawut said, baffled.

"What? Don't you remember me, Chan, you old bugger? Your old mate Liam, we were soldiers together! Yes! They made me headman, but don't worry, don't feel intimidated. You and me, we're old friends. Let's keep going as we were then, I won't mind. Have a seat!" Headman Liam poured a glass of whisky and pushed it over to him. "Have a gulp of this, then you can tell me where you've been hiding out."

THAT night, in the boat on his way home, Surawut made a firm decision to entrust his son to the care of his uncle Pan, so as not to be a burden on him. Because he was going to have to tear himself away to try his luck or chance his fate elsewhere . . . He could not stay in the village any longer. How could he, when the appellation 'Chan, you old bastard', which he had thought dead, came frighteningly to life so soon after 'Chan' and 'Uncle Chan'. Before he left that night, Liam had promised repeatedly to spread the word among his contemporaries that they should get together for a drinking session to welcome the old bastard Chan home.

TWO nights later, Lieutenant-Colonel Surawut travelled back to Bangkok by passenger boat. When the ferry left Ban Phaen that night, he sat quietly on the bench at the prow close to the steersman. He listened to the rain falling resoundingly on the roof of the boat and the surface of the water, and tried to resolve a number of problems . . . Rain was water which had condensed and risen, but it had to return inevitably to its original condition with the other drops of water. But he was not water. He was a living, breathing person. When fate decreed that he should float to the upper regions, how could he then flow back to his former level? No matter what, he would have to keep struggling. For honour . . . his hard won honour.

And so death, which came to so many others in that boat when it capsized, came to adjust the level of his life, unasked.

Next morning a middle-aged villager looked searchingly on Surawut's face as his body lay on the bank, then turned to a young deputy district officer walking by and said, "Deputy . . . Deputy Sir! I know this bloke well. He was a soldier with me way back then! He lives just out of Phak Hai. His name was . . . was . . . hang on, it's on the tip of my tongue . . .

Oh! I remember now, his name was Chan, the old bastard!"

THONGPROI—THE RICH GIRL

THONGPROI was aware that she was extremely fortunate. She had never experienced the suffering which comes from deprivation or unfulfilled desire. Even though she was the youngest daughter in the large family of a couple running a business in Chao Chet, Thongproi had always received special attention from her parents and her elder siblings. She was, after all, the youngest; and she had been so ill when she was little that her parents had despaired of her life. But she had survived miraculously. Moreover, her parents believed that their youngest daughter had brought good fortune to the family— ever since her birth her parents' business had boomed, and now they were reputed to be the most prosperous family in the district.

For these reasons, Thongproi was born into a world full of people ready to pander to her every whim. She got everything she wanted, because none of her elder brothers or sisters ever opposed her. When she wanted something that was going to be expensive, her parents did not refuse but said instead, "Let Proi have what she wants. We owe her our fortune, she brought it with her when she was born. She must have made merit in her previous incarnation. There's no point regretting the expense."

No-one ever opposed any of Thongproi's demands in childhood. Whether it was food, toys or clothes, she only had to ask and it would be hers. She enjoyed a happy childhood, as her childish wants were easily satisfied. The family never let her ask twice for anything, and she was content with the knowledge that all her wants would be met. Lying in bed under her mosquito net, she sometimes thought, as children do, about all the things she still wanted, and made a mental note to tell her parents the next day. She would fall asleep then, secure in the certainty that she would have no problem getting them.

Had Thongproi been able to remain in a state of perpetual childhood, or had her demands never gone beyond childish whims, she might never have had to suffer.

THONGPROI grew up to be one of the most beautiful young women in the district. Her parents took greater care of her than ever. Because of her family's wealth, her natural beauty never needed to be marred by exposure to the elements, or the need to do the ordinary tasks usually undertaken by girls of her age. Her parents' meticulous care, protection, and indulgence had bestowed on her the reputation of a beauty. Apart from her physical qualities, it was known that as a millionaire's daughter she was materially well endowed. With these two points in her favour, Thongproi should have been an object of interest to numerous young men, but every time anyone mentioned her name in connection with marriage, someone would say, "The likes of you or I wouldn't be able to provide for her. That Proi's parents didn't bring her up like everyone else. They've indulged her since childhood, never reproached or scolded her, and always given her everything she wanted. She's never done a stroke of work—she couldn't even so much as steam rice or boil soup. They've always been rich enough to hire servants for all that. When people like us marry, our wives have to help us earn a living. If you took a wife who did nothing but sleep and eat, and you had to indulge her whims like her parents did, it'd be like bringing somebody into the house simply to take command, and who could put up with that?"

Observations like this discouraged the young men, who wanted their wives to share their work as well as leisure. So even though Thongproi was blossoming into womanhood, no-one showed any interest in her. Knowing that she was used to a lifestyle beyond their means and status, none of the village elders had singled her out for a marriage proposal with their sons. As for Thongproi herself, she was not interested in these matters. Although her needs had changed with maturity, the need for love and a marriage partner had not yet emerged. Her parents, too, had other plans for her. They wanted her to be better educated than themselves and to have a higher position in the world. One of her father's cousins was a senior government official in Bangkok. She was sent to live with him to further her education and practice a 'civilized' lifestyle, to mix with people of name and fame, and to learn the rules of behaviour and etiquette favoured by high society.

LIFE in Bangkok did not excite Thongproi as it should have done. From the time she could read, and first developed an interest in the world around her, she had used all her spare time in the leisurely manner of a millionaire's daughter. She had read books and magazines from Bangkok, most of which, naturally, were about Bangkok's people, its life and atmosphere. Thong-proi knew more about Bangkok than anyone else in the district, and had built up an image of it in her mind. Even before she had ever been there she dressed and behaved as a Bangkok girl would, following what she had read and heard of from city visitors.

When she finally got there, she was not greatly impressed, and even a little disappointed. The real Bangkok lacked the splendour and sparkle of the city of her imagination. Yet she was not greatly upset either, because she had only to reach for a piece of paper and write a letter home, for her parents to send money by return mail for whatever it was she wanted in Bangkok—clothes, cosmetics, or money for entertainment. She hardly even needed to remind them.

Possessing money, the most important means of leading a life of independence and self-indulgence, Thongproi failed to realize its true value. And naturally, life soon became bland and boring. Life in Bangkok, which should have meant so much to Thongproi, became instead insipid and flavourless. Although she clutched at everything she had ever heard existed there—cinema, theatre, shops, fairs and parties—and although the relatives she stayed with had children around her own age, who were her companions in eating, gadding about, and spending money, it was not long before these pleasures began to pall from sheer familiarity. Jaded, Thongproi saw Bangkok as empty and meaningless. The subjects her relatives suggested she take up—domestic science, sewing—did not interest her. She saw no need to acquire such skills. Why should she learn house-keeping, when there were others to do it for her? Why should she learn dressmaking when she could always pay someone else to do it better? Thongproi began to yearn for a life free from boredom, something more enjoyable than she had previously experienced. Before she left home, she had imagined she would find this in Bangkok, but after living there she realized that her hopes were not to be fulfilled. Life in Bangkok was as boring as it was at home. Thongproi was still too inexperienced to know that happiness and suffering were relative. Excessive happiness, unrestrained indulgence, and constant fulfilment of her every want had, in the end, deprived her life of all meaning.

The hopes of the poor or the luckless contain the possibility of eventual satisfaction, but the deep-seated malaise of the person who has everything is harder by far to cure. When Thongproi finally despaired of finding anything more to do in Bangkok, she decided to return home. The decision once made, she packed her belongings, said farewell to her friends and relatives, and set off home by boat, refusing to be dissuaded. She did not know that her relatives had written to her parents complaining bitterly of her selfishness and refusal to listen to the advice of her elders. Her parents did not reproach her, as it had become habitual with them to let her have her own way.

On the boat trip back from Bangkok, Thongproi became aware that the young man beside her was taking an intense interest in her. He was about her age, or not more than three years older, handsome, polite, and well-groomed. She learnt from the nametag on the large suitcase by his side that his name was San, and that he was a deputy district officer of her own district. She guessed immediately, both from his behaviour and because she had never seen him in the area before, that he must be travelling to take up duty. As the boat moved steadily away from Bangkok, San frequently glanced at Thongproi. Seeing that she seemed agreeable to making his acquaintance, he introduced himself before the boat reached the junction. By the time it had turned into the waterway and was moving past the paddy fields, he had begun to tell her his life story. He told her he was from Bangkok, and that this was the first time he had been out to the provinces on an official posting. He felt very nervous, as well as excited, but had accepted because it meant a promotion. The two of them sat chatting on about various things. San agreed with whatever opinion she expressed. By the time the boat reached Ban Praen, Thongproi knew her own mind. She wanted San to be her life's partner. It could not be said that Thongproi's feelings were those of love at first sight, or of love borne of compassion, and certainly they did not represent love flowing from mutual sympathy. All Thongproi knew was that she wanted him to belong to her just as she had wanted, and got, possession of so many other things in the past. As San's looks and manner of speaking were to her liking, she wanted him for those same reasons, unaware that at the same time he had fallen hopelessly in love with her, with a love which could only continue to grow, and which would never diminish.

When Thongproi's fancy coincided with San's falling madly in love with her from their first meeting, it was not surprising that he was a frequent visitor. Over the next seven months, her indulgent parents organized an ostentatious wedding for them and built a modern house near to their own for the young couple, decked out with any expensive items she happened to fancy. They also provided a substantial sum of money to start them off, without asking for anything in exchange from the groom.

Thongproi experienced untold happiness in the first year of marriage. Her life was now fulfilled, as her husband had become the focus of the interest and desire she had previously lacked. She wanted nothing other than him, and he surrendered himself to her completely. He was a hundred times more indulgent than her parents. She wanted for nothing, and he carried out her every wish. He even did all the little household things she should have done for him, as if he were one of the two servants she had hired to do her bidding. Everyone who saw Thongproi's marriage said that she was incredibly lucky and, for the first year, she agreed with them.

In fact, the early stages of Thongproi's married life were so smooth and free from difficulties that she began to tire of it as she had of everything else before. Her husband's readiness to grant her every whim would have been gratifying had it been a novelty. No obstacle ever seemed to hinder the even course of the marriage. San showed no sign of changing. The more Thongproi reflected on her life, the more bored she became, and having once admitted that boredom she found that it gathered force with every passing day. Her life was like that of a caged bird with a conscientious keeper. She wanted for nothing. She encountered no dangers, felt no suffering, took no risks, and was without hopes or worries. Life flowed on abundantly. She got everything she wanted, as she always had. San did everything she told him to. Life was becoming flat and insipid again, devoid of the sadness or anxiety that made times of happiness and freedom from care appear all the more brilliant by contrast.

Thongproi spent most of her time sitting at the front of the house watching the boats pass up and down the waterway. Poor couples rowed past, their faces burnt by the sun. Although they wore ragged clothes and their faces were lined with the marks of their harsh existence, she glimpsed flashes of a happiness which eluded her. Sometimes the riverboat couples would moor their loaded boats by the bank near her house. Occasionally she heard the sounds of quarrels and fights, which made her think that maybe conflict and disagreement between lovers was like a spice, or sharp curry paste, which added pungency to an otherwise monotonous diet. She had been unable to add savour to her own life in this way, because her husband took no notice of the wiles she used to try to pick quarrels with him. He was always the first to make up and placate her, which forced her to shed bitter tears over the loneliness and monotony of her life.

San had a group of friends, most of whom had been at school with him. All were young and dashing, and most did not have families of their own. Whenever one of them passed through the district he stayed with San, so Thongproi came to know them too. She was a beautiful woman, and it was natural that some of the young men could not resist taking an interest in her. To enliven her existence, she went out of her way to attract those who came to stay for any length of time, but far from becoming possessive or standing in her way, San pretended not to notice. At times he even seemed to encourage her to associate with other men. As time went on, his generosity of spirit made her increasingly resentful. She came to regard her husband as of little importance, like a piece of furniture which had outlived its day and needed to be stored away. Still, because he was indeed not an inanimate object but a person, and her husband in name at least, she had to endure a life now totally devoid of meaning.

Most people would have envied her lot, because she always had her way. But life without passion or suffering is inevitably trivial. Having always got everything she wanted, she began to long for the impossible. She wanted San to oppose her and take advantage of her, like men in novels she had read, but he did not. It would have gone against his habitual indulgence of her every wish.

In the third year of marriage, Thongproi fell prey to ill health. San and her relatives took her to goodness knows how many doctors, but her symptoms proved quite intractable. The truth of the matter was, life contained nothing which made her wish to prolong it. The mixture of happiness and sorrow that made up most people's lives was not for Thongproi, who had everything anyone could ever want—money, a house, and an attentive husband. People could not imagine what more she could possibly want. She herself did not know the answer to this question. So it was that she gradually lost the will to go on living from day to day. Finally, San decided to take leave and to accompany his wife to Bangkok for treatment, thinking that a change of scene and a chance of some outings might alleviate her symptoms.

THONGPROI sat silently in the boat with San. When it left Ban Phaen that evening she let her thoughts wander and mingle with the sounds of the rain and thunderstorm around her. San was speaking softly to her, but she was not listening. He was probably asking whether she wanted anything, so he could get it for her as he always did, but Thongproi was overcome by a profound distaste for everything. There was nothing more that she wanted.

No-one could say how many more years Thongproi would have endured her sterile existence had the boat not overturned. She was sitting staring into space as if only half awake when the boat keeled to one side and capsized. San was flung violently in another direction. When she hit the surface of the water Thongproi let herself sink without making the slightest effort to save herself.

Looking on the face of his lifeless wife at dawn next morning, after the villagers had raised her dead body from the river, San noticed that her eyes were shut and there was a smile playing around her lips. It was the way she used to look whenever he brought her something she particularly wanted, or did exactly what she wished.

SAENG—THE DOCTOR

FROM the time Saeng could understand, he saw death as an enemy to be fought unremittingly. This was not because he was born with any particular disease, or so weak that he might die at any moment. On the contrary, he was strong and healthy, and could hope to live as long as any other child. Yet because his father was a doctor, he regarded death as the ultimate enemy confronting him, against whom he must wage perpetual warfare.

His father, Doctor Sut, was well known in Tung Sano subdistrict in the Suphan region where Saeng was born. From earliest childhood, Saeng saw his father perform feats of combat against death and disease. Saeng was close to his father. His first memories were of the familiar aroma of herbal medicines. Later his father taught him to understand the essentials of traditional medicine. At first he only helped pound the ingre-dients and shape them into tablets, but in time he learnt to distinguish between the various kinds and categories of herbs, knowing which were 'hot', which 'cold', and all the other properties of each one.

IN those days, people still depended on traditional doctors and herbal medicines to cure disease. Saeng recalled distinctly that there were fewer diseases around in those days. All his father's patients, if they did not have colds, had fevers from the onset of the cool season, or wasting diseases or various skin parasites. An examination of the symptoms and a small dose of medicine usually cured them. No-one knew about injections, or took western medicine. But diseases were few, with none of the strange new illnesses we have today. When Saeng grew up, he studied the medical and medicinal treatises with his father, and knew all the diseases contained therein. He knew which foods exacerbated which diseases; that 'hot' medicine cured wind whereas delicate 'cold' medicines were used for fever; which fevers needed laxatives or purgatives; how to prepare children's dosages and treat infant ailments; and how to alter the liquid content of the medicine in order to cure a range of diseases. But what Doctor Sut was most emphatic about were the ideals and duties of a doctor. He often said to his son, "Other ways of earning a living are all very well—but when you prosper and you don't do anything for anyone else… and there's so much sickness and disease around, and . . . we're all members of the human race. Saeng, my boy! If there were no doctors and no medicine, wouldn't everyone be dead by now? Sure, you could say it's not bad being a doctor—people everywhere respect you, doctors only have friends, never enemies—but it is also enormously wearing. People who work on the land, in business, or in other occupa-tions have regular hours, and when they're tired they can sleep or rest to regain their strength. But not doctors. They don't stop, they keep going, day and night. Sickness and disease and the lord of death wait for no-one. We doctors have to fight them first to help our fellows."

Another thing his father often said was, "If you want to be rich, don't consider being a doctor. Think about it—greedy people, only interested in making a fortune, aren't to be trusted with matters of life and death. The patient's life is in the hands of the doctor. If the doctor is motivated by greed, what a terrible risk the patient takes! I think the ancient masters must have felt this way, when they laid down in the texts that fees were not to be more than a *salung* or *baht* at a time. A packet of medicine was only a *phai* or a *fuang*, a potion was ten *salung* or three *baht* at most, and one pot sufficed as a cure. Sums of hundreds and thousands never came the way of a doctor, Saeng, so think carefully. For myself, I love the profession. Even if I'm not as rich as others I see it as accumulating merit for helping my fellows. If you see someone lying ill and immobilised with fever, and you help them to get on their feet and regain their old strength, it gives you much more of a lift than money . . . "

Saeng recognized the truth in his father's words. He was fully aware that people from all around the district looked up to and respected Doctor Sut. In fact, his father's income was quite low, as he said, but Saeng never felt that his family had suffered hardship. When fully recovered, patients who had paid only a pittance for the doctor's services often showed their gratitude with payment in kind—vegetables, fish or fruit. Saeng's family always had enough to live on, and never went without.

Saeng studied his father's profession intently. Seeing his interest, Doctor Sut taught him all he knew. Saeng studied the texts his father had collected over the years, and expanded the horizons of his knowledge. As he grew older, he visited patients with his father, noting the various symptoms and their treatment, down to the medicines prescribed. Eventually Doctor Sut began to allow Saeng to treat patients on his own. The locals called him 'Doctor Saeng'.

Doctor Saeng differed sharply from his father in his attitude to death. Many of the patients they treated were cured, but some died. Every time a patient seemed beyond hope, Doctor Sut packed up his medicine and left the house, a sign of defeat. But Doctor Saeng stayed to fight death until the end. He refused to give in, no matter how dire the condition. Doctor Sut could accept a patient's death, but Doctor Saeng had never been able to. He felt sorry every time a patient died, and humiliated at his defeat, even though Doctor Sut reminded him that death was an inevitable part of life's cycle which, when the time came, could not be stopped by any number of doctors or any amount of medicine.

Doctor Saeng could not share his father's acceptance of death's inevitability. He did not believe that it was a matter of fate. In his eyes, death was the enemy, a rival to outwit and outsmart. Death was the victor when a patient died, and Doctor Saeng felt shame and distress at his defeat. This could make him upset or uneasy for days on end. And the more he felt this way, the more death became an adversary against whom he sought vengeance. Death was like a personal opponent playing secret games with him, ever lying in wait to prevent his actions from reaching fruition.

The perception of a contest between himself on the one hand, and death on the other, spurred him to fight to the end in the hope of final victory.He learnt all his father's texts by heart, then began to look around for others. If ever he heard that anyone had effective medicine, he managed to obtain some and made it his own, analysing its properties according to the principles he had learnt from books newly acquired. He would not place immediate faith in it, and used it on his patients only after he had judged it suitable for treating the disease it purported to cure. Then he followed the symptoms keenly to see what benefits the medicine had wrought. Each medicine was a weapon in his duel, and new medicines were yet another addition to his armoury. If the new formula worked, and the patient recovered, he was pleased and satisfied with his victory. He had no interest in payment for medicines or treatment. Doctor Saeng became known as a doctor who treated patients for merit rather than personal gain. No-one understood that he was fighting a battle, locked in mortal combat with a foe and rival whom he had never seen, although he knew it lay in wait to seize the advantage at every possible turn. Whenever he deprived his enemy of that opportunity he knew he had won, and felt greater pride and pleasure than if he had been paid in gold.

THE day finally came when his rival, closing in, drove the attack home. Ageing Doctor Sut fell ill with bouts of heavy wheezing. After a couple of days he said to his son, "Saeng, this time there's no cure. You're my only son, and fully grown now, too. Guard the knowledge I've passed on to you once I'm gone, it's the only property I have to leave you . . . "

"But, Father," Doctor Saeng protested, but Doctor Sut interrupted him saying, "Don't argue with me. I know I won't make it this time, with these symptoms. My time has come—don't waste money on medicine for me. I've been treating patients for years—some of them recovered, others didn't. I know all about it . . . life and death . . . I know when my time has come."

Doctor Sut began gasping for breath. Doctor Saeng had to prop him up hurriedly so he could breathe more easily, cutting off any further opportunity for discussion of the subject.

Nevertheless, Doctor Saeng refused to heed his father's words. Not only was his father so ill that he had to devote all his skills to treating him, but as well he felt that this time the enemy had attacked with impunity on his home ground. He had to fight back as best he could, to avoid simply conceding defeat. He used all available medication to treat his father's illness and sat observing his father's symptoms day and night without pausing for sleep. Yet he fought alone, without his father's co-operation. Doctor Sut sometimes took the medicine, but at other times he refused. Indeed, he showed every sign of welcoming death, the deadly enemy, and of admitting defeat instead of fighting back. At times Doctor Saeng felt hurt and angry, as though his father who had joined him for so long in his struggle against the enemy, had defected to the other side.

Doctor Sut died after Doctor Saeng had devoted every ounce of his strength and skill to his care for seven days. A few hours before his death he had warned his son, as he gasped for breath, "I told you . . . Saeng . . . curing disease is like a war. If we win, well and good, but we have to admit defeat when we're done. You have to have the right attitude . . . This time I've lost . . . but you're still there . . . keep on fighting, Saeng . . . but if you win, don't get cocky . . . and don't lose heart if you're beaten."

His father's death made Doctor Saeng even more ruthless. He was fighting a vendetta with death as if it were a person who had caused him suffering and deep pain. He was prepared to sacrifice his entire life to the struggle. A small voice within him kept whispering that in the end, he would be the loser, but he ignored it. Quite the contrary—he began to think ahead to new weapons he could use to produce better results, for instance a longevity medicine that could prolong life, health and strength. He had heard that the formula for this elixir was buried deep in a secret text and spent all the time he could spare from caring for his patients in journeying from place to place in search of it.

Every word Doctor Sut had said about medicine as a profession was true. Doctor Saeng was no richer or better off, and if anything, was worse off, than when his father was alive. Doctor Sut had had an established reputation. While Doctor Saeng was well received if sent to a case in his stead, with some of Doctor Sut's patients staying on after his death, quite a few left for other doctors and treatments. His moderate income fell; his standard of living dropped. Had he been a bachelor and living alone he might not have worried or even noticed, but he was not. Before his father's death he had married a woman named Plang, a distant relative. The marriage had been arrang-ed by their elders, and they led an unexceptional life.

Plang was rather a good-looking woman. Like most attractive people, she hoped for and demanded from life a living standard to match her looks. In a sense she loved Doctor Saeng, the way every woman loves her husband. But his way of earning a living to support his family was not at all to her taste. She did not see that he gained merit by treating patients; she saw no value in presenting offerings to the masters, objects declared sacred by preceptors of old; she did not care about a doctor's duty or the trust and respect it could bring. She regarded medicine as the kind of profession which should be amply recompensed. To her, medicines were merely goods, products, and the more profit that could be made from them the better. When it became clear that Doctor Saeng was not interested in payment for either treatment or medicine, and sometimes even wore himself out treating a patient for nothing, she thought him a fool. She saw him as stupid and slow, forever allowing himself to be duped and used and never any better off.

Plang's views were diametrically opposed to Doctor Saeng's, which led to disagreement and frequent quarrels. She did most of the quarrelling, going on endlessly about poverty and hardship and blaming him for everything. He remained silent. After a while she saw that her verbal assaults would not alter his character, and so decided to take over the business herself.

She dealt with his patients directly. If he was in his room, she sat at the front of the house and told the poorer patients that he was out. If he could be seen, and she could not pretend he was not there, her looks and actions would indicate that poor patients were not welcome. Plang took over the distribution of the medicine, arguing that it relieved her husband of the burden. Then she priced it as she pleased—sometimes on a whim, sometimes greedily.

Doctor Saeng paid no attention to what she did. As time went on he lost interest in his surroundings. He went on treating patients because it was part of his daily routine. He used standard medicines, no longer motivated to seek additional knowledge but obsessed with a single thought—the weapon he would use to avenge his enemy, death. The weapon he was seeking so determinedly was the medicine of longevity. He collected numerous texts on life-prolonging medicines from a variety of places, and proceeded to study and experiment. When he had collected all of the ingredients he tried them out himself. Some medicines had no effect, and left him feeling the same as ever; some drugs contained poisons from obscure herbs, which made him drunk, or caused violent stomach upsets, itchy rashes, or blisters. None of this deterred him as he had given himself over to fighting the unbeatable foe.

Plang's activities did not help. The low income she tried to augment kept falling, because regular patients stayed away, put off by her greed. Yet had she done nothing the result would have been much the same. The era of modern medicine had dawned, and the days of the medical profession to which Doctor Saeng belonged were numbered. Medicines which treated disease more effectively than herbal remedies were readily available, as were patent medicines for fever, diarrhoea, worms, and many other ailments. These were sold by the boatload, and advertised by recorded jingles which played day and night. Patients could administer the medicines themselves, and no longer needed a doctor for minor illnesses. Apart from that, there were modern doctors, or people who styled themselves as such, going around treating patients by injections, more effectively and vigorously than the old method of boiling up a potion.

For these reasons, Doctor Saeng's status fell from that of a 'doctor' who catered to society's essential needs, to that of a 'practitioner of ancient medicine', a relic of a bygone era. All he represented now was an occasional alternative treatment for those who refused to move with the times.

Doctor Saeng was not aware of these things, or if he was, he showed no interest. He continued his struggle, confident that one day he would win. Plang had to go into business to alleviate their hardships. She sold off the old things in the house to buy other goods to resell at a profit, to sustain their existence from day to day.

MANY years passed. Doctor Saeng was still preoccupied with mixing medicines and experimenting with various formulae he managed to obtain. One day, gazing fixedly ahead as he chopped some dried medicinal ingredients, he thought about the properties of some medicines he was currently keen on. Lost in thought, he came to his senses when the dry ingredients he had been chopping became wet and soggy for no apparent reason. He bent down quickly to look. His heart missed a beat when he saw that his hand, and the chopped ingredients, were soaked in fresh blood. He had accidentally chopped the top off his index finger, a deep wound. The blood was still gushing. He got up hurriedly and washed his hand to cleanse the blood from his finger, quickly found some medicine to stem the flow, and bandaged it with a cloth. It was then that he began to wonder, with amazement, why he had not felt instant pain when the knife sliced a large gash in his finger, but had kept on chopping more and more ingredients until he sensed that the ingredients were soaking wet. His amazement turned to suspicion when he washed his hands, and felt no pain when he pressed heavily on the cut.

"Perhaps it's the effect of the medicine I took this morning," he muttered to himself. "Strange, very strange—if such a deep cut still doesn't hurt there might be some value in it."

The cut healed rapidly, yet Doctor Saeng began to sense a numbness at his fingertips, so that he could barely feel whatever he touched. He observed his symptoms with increasing curiosity.

Another day he had set up a small stove and was boiling water. He picked up a book to read while he waited, and became so absorbed that he forgot about the fire in front of him. He could not remember how long he had sat there reading, but at one point he had stretched out his legs and bent forward. He was alerted when he caught the smell of burning flesh, as though someone were grilling meat nearby. Raising his head from the book, he took a sniff and looked around. That instant his hair stood on end in horror and he quickly drew his feet back. His big toe had touched against the hot stove, and remained there until he caught the whiff of burning flesh.

From that time on, Doctor Saeng began to worry about his bodily condition, as if it held hidden secrets which he wished to suppress all knowledge of. For months he refused to allow himself to believe that he was stricken with a dire illness. There came a day, however, when his secret became too obvious to hide any longer. When he looked into the mirror to brush his hair after a wash, he saw clear signs of leprosy on his face and the edges of his earlobes. From whom he had caught it, or when, he had no way of knowing. Looking at his face, he noticed that the tip of his nose was becoming thinner and the bridge flatter. He sighed deeply as he scrutinized his features. He was about to experience the biggest defeat of his life.

True, leprosy was not a disease which brought instant death upon its sufferers, but with such an affliction death was never far away. Such parts of the body as fingertips, toes and ears, gradually deteriorated and shrank, and were not replaced. The skin on Doctor Saeng's hands and feet became dessicated, and felt increasingly stunted, like dried leather, or wood or inanimate iron. No new flesh replaced that which was dying. His enemy had attacked not to claim victory but to taunt him with its silent presence within him. Instead of wresting a decisive victory, death invaded the person of Doctor Saeng in order to make itself manifest. No longer did it conceal itself waiting for an opening.

Afflicted with these symptoms, he began to look around him. For the first time he took stock of his own position, and saw that he was a poor man without wealth or possessions to live off once he became unable to treat patients. When Plang saw his symptoms, and eventually found out that her husband had leprosy, she was openly repulsed. The constant criticism that he had become accustomed to increased daily, as if the enormity of his fate were his own fault. She made him move out to the tumbledown shack at the back of the house, and put leftover scraps out for his meals. News spread through the neighbourhood that Doctor Saeng no longer cured disease, but was himself a carrier—a leper.

He was alone in the midst of humanity. Everywhere he went people avoided him, out of revulsion, because his face, hands, feet, and skin bore the clear marks of leprosy. True, those who were unaware of his history might not have noticed much difference between him and anyone else, but people in the same neighbourhood of the same small district all knew, and knowing, tended to exaggerate. Doctor Saeng had time now to ponder on himself and his relation to the world, and the more he thought, the more his ideas and feelings changed.

He no longer hated death or regarded it as the enemy. It was not something against which he had to engage in a constant battle of wits, as in the past. On reflection, he saw death as a wondrous thing, a needed friend. Death would come as an act of compassion rather than an enactment of the final victory. He began to invite death, to pray for it to come quickly, instead of contemplating fighting or avoiding it, as he had done all his life. Yet death appeared satisfied with manifesting itself through his living tissues, and was not in any hurry to attack with its final act of power, as he wished it would.

As time passed, the symptoms of the disease became increasingly obvious. Doctor Saeng began to dream of seeking refuge where he was unknown. He knew that if he stayed he could not bear for much longer the changes, the aloofness, and the signs of revulsion from former friends. His symptoms did not cause particular pain, but the comments of acquaintances made his heart ache. When the death he yearned for showed no sign of coming, he decided to take refuge elsewhere. He would go where nobody knew him, where nobody was interested, and he could go wherever he liked . . .

THAT night Doctor Saeng boarded the boat with no destination in mind. He knew it was heading for Bangkok, but he did not want to go there. The place he wanted was far from the crowds of Bangkok . . . but Bangkok, or anywhere for that matter, was better than home. When he heard the sound of the alarm, the rain pounding on the roof of the boat and the surface of the water, he pulled aroundhim more closely the cloth he used to cover his face and body to prevent people from seeing clearly the marks of his disease. Within the boat it was murky. Darkness enveloped the river and waterways. He breathed a long sigh of relief. Darkness was an ornament which could adorn him temporarily to make him an ordinary person on an equal plane with others. Nobody could see him in the dark, but when light dawned he was a leper again, and people avoided contact with him.

In the dawn light next morning, no-one would go near Doctor Saeng's body, lying on the riverbank, because it was the body of a leper. Even so, those who passed at a distance could not help noticing that the wide-open eyes of the corpse reflected a glimmer of happiness. It was as if, before dying, he had met his long-awaited beloved—directly and unexpectedly, face-to-face.

EPILOGUE

MANY lives . . . many different lives. Different in age, in sex, in occupation. But all drowned together, in the same place, in the same way, and at the same time. Who could have been the judge, the arbiter, to say what *karma* caused things to turn out in such a way?

Karma is for all of us the starting-point of birth and the preserver of life, and by the same token, leads us to our end. But what sort of a *karma* could it have been that brought death to so many people at the same time?

All that most of us ordinary mortals, who are not the Lord Brahma, can see is just the one thing: which is that death, so much feared by us all, can in some cases be a dreadful punishment for wrongdoing, in some cases a reward for virtue; in others, the solution to a problem, or in still others, a healing balm for a wound unable to be healed by any other means.

Many lives ended together, lives that had loved, loathed, laughed and cried, been sad and happy. But was that really the end? The sun still shone and sparkled on the dewy grass along the riverbank, and the foliage still gleamed with life, a witness to hope. That river still flowed relentlessly on, flowed on towards the vast ocean. As long as it was there, boats would ply up and down endlessly, as with the river of life which flows to all eternity. When there is birth, it is followed by death, and then there must be birth again. The only people who can escape being swallowed up by that river are those who are able to swim ashore and find a dry spot on the bank on which to stand, refusing to allow themselves to be carried away by the river of life. But, caught in the torrential currents of life's river, who among us is capable of doing such a thing?